THE MYTHS OF MANIFESTING

7 Hidden Blocks Stopping Your Manifestation
Success and How to Remove Them

Mistakes and Misconceptions
Around Reality Creation

Ryuu Shinohara

Omen
Publishing

HOW TO GET THE MOST
OUT OF THIS BOOK

I see it all the time. People read LOA book after LOA book without ever taking action on any of the insights they've gained or concepts they've learned. The last thing I want is for you to read this book, forget everything you read, and continue to live as you've lived. You picked this book up for a reason: to manifest positive change. These additional resources will help you along this journey.

>> Scan the QR Code to gain exclusive access
to these resources <<

Free Bonus #1: Manifestor Masterlist

In this document, you'll discover the top 3 daily habits for manifesting a life beyond your wildest dreams. Includes a simple layout to track your progress and instructions to get started today.

Free Bonus #2: Intention Journal

Journaling doesn't need to take 10 minutes away from your morning routine. In fact, if you structure it right, you can get it done in under a minute. This intention journal focuses on the essential components that make this practice so powerful.

Free Bonus #3: 4 Subtle Meditation Mistakes to Avoid

A deep meditative state can be challenging to come by. The mind and body will do everything possible to stop you from fully surrendering. If you truly want to maximize the benefits of your meditation practice, check out this document to avoid making the same mistakes millions are making.

Free Bonus #4: Meditation Design

There are many different ways to meditate. After testing many other methods, I've put together a step-by-step structure that I've found to be the most effective for deepening your state and embodying the future you.

Free Bonus #5: 4-Step Conscious Business Acceleration

Being an entrepreneur and business owner comes with many unique challenges and struggles. In this document, we'll tackle the top 3 blocks that are stopping most people from experiencing quantum leaps in their financial and business ventures.

Free Bonus #6: Vision Calendar

Are you struggling with consistency and clarity? The Vision Calendar is tailored to outline your daily/monthly/quarterly/yearly goals and intentions into bite-size pieces to prevent overwhelm and confusion.

Free Bonus #7: 4 Anti-Manifestation Practices

Sometimes people make mistakes. That's okay. Other times, they unconsciously sabotage themselves without even knowing it. This document will outline commonly taught manifestation practices that work against you and how to shift them to your benefit.

To get your free bonuses go to:

https://monkmodeuniversity.ck.page/mmybonuses

Or scan the QR Code below

Table of Contents

Introduction

You set your intentions. You did the work. You maintained the attitude. You believed with every ounce of your being and still… *nothing*!

"What am I doing wrong?"

This question is often murmured by those who attempt to manifest a better reality, only to find more of the same, or a mutant version of their desires manifested. As a result, they feel disappointment, frustration, doubt, and a lack of self-confidence.

If this resonates with you, I'd like to invite you to consider the following: What if *you* didn't do anything wrong?

What if you're following exactly what you learned about the Law of Attraction, and you still aren't achieving results? What if what you learned about the Law of Attraction was incomplete or misinterpreted by you or your teacher?

Would you still feel the disappointment, frustration, or lack of self-confidence if you knew that *you* weren't the problem, but rather, your approach was?

Odds are that you would probably still feel frustrated with the time and energy you spent doing things the 'wrong' way. However, at least your inner critic would be much quieter. If there was some critical piece of information that was missing, then you can't beat yourself up about your inability to manifest your desired results.

Getting frustrated at yourself in this scenario would be similar to buying a new five-thousand-piece puzzle set, only to find a portion of the pieces missing, and then blaming yourself for the missing pieces. If you're working with an incomplete picture, you can't blame yourself for the inability to complete it, just as you can't blame the person who sold you the set, who thought all the pieces were inside the box.

Misinterpretation is the vulnerability of language, words, and communication. It is the result of trying to logically interpret information, as opposed to relating to it at the level intended by the person portraying the message. When the discussion is around invisible concepts like spirituality and metaphysics, misinterpretations and mistakes become even more common.

Fortunately, there is a solution to this problem. If you purchased a puzzle set with missing pieces, you can simply go back to the store and exchange it for a complete set. Yes, there is some effort in going back to the store, retracing your steps, and making the exchange, but in the end, you'll have a complete set. You'll be able to achieve your goals and manifest the reality you envisioned because you'll have everything you need—and *don't* need—to guide you there.

The Law of Attraction has a massive audience that seeks to learn everything there is to know about the subject. They read books, take courses, watch videos, and attend seminars, yet there are still so many people who find it difficult to truly embody the concepts. I've received many emails myself. While it's impossible for me to

address all of their problems personally and at a deep level, I have come to figure out exactly what the problem is.

Despite all the information out there, there are many seekers who still seem to struggle with the Law of Attraction, or at the very least, struggle to achieve a state of inner peace with themselves and their environment—knowing and having faith that things will work out eventually. This is when I decided to take on the task of 'clearing the air.'

During my time writing, I have managed to comb through thousands of emails and messages from readers, to the point when I began to see the patterns. It often isn't the material that is presented that is in question, but rather the ideas, beliefs, and concepts that many seekers thought to be true but were actually a warped version of the truth, due to ways the concepts were presented to them.

The truth of the matter is that the Law of Attraction can be difficult to understand conceptually, as it is experienced differently from person to person. We sometimes believe that we know about a concept, but we do not realize that we don't truly understand the truth behind it. This isn't a reflection on one's intelligence or ability to learn; it could be simple misconceptions or assumptions influenced by culture, education, and other factors.

Science, for example, is something that most people trust. We constantly hear it said to "trust the science!" Yet, even within this alleged safe space of truth, we can find misconceptions and mistakes frequently.

Take the following statement: "Science is a collection of facts." What was your initial reaction when you read the statement? Did you believe it to be true or false?

Most of us would have leaned toward it being true. However, this is a common misconception about science. While it is true that science does involve collecting data which are presented as facts, the truth is that science is a body of knowledge constantly undergoing a process of change.

The facts of science are subject to be proven incorrect as new data continues to emerge. There was a time when it was scientifically accurate to say that the sun revolved around the Earth, until Galileo disproved it. Today, if you were to claim that the sun revolves around the earth, you'd be laughed at by a group of kindergarteners. The facts changed, and the body of knowledge evolved. Science isn't a collection of facts; it's a continuous process of learning and growth.

Misconceptions, as a whole, can influence our reality, limiting our ability to evolve beyond what we deem to be true. Could you imagine trying to attempt space travel under the premise that the Earth is flat or that the sun revolves around the Earth? It would be catastrophic!

Misinterpreted information is why, many times, people who attempt to use the Law of Attraction to manifest their best lives often fall flat on their faces. When the information in books, courses, speeches, and articles revolves around concepts such as manifesting, it means something different to every person reading it, thus leaving room for different interpretations. Fortunately, there are ways of reducing this.

There are infinite models to describe reality. No one book or lesson can ever represent the 'ultimate truth.' However, through personal experience and self-reflection, we can begin building up a collection of subtle nuances we can use to further tweak our approach to manifesting.

While my other books were all about how to manifest and use the Law of Attraction in a more practical sense using one model, this book is dedicated to uncovering the misconceptions and myths that keep many people from misinterpreting the content and feeling stuck in their journeys. It is for those who understand that the Law of Attraction works, but who simply can't seem to fine-tune their manifesting abilities or feel that they are getting less than what they initially intended.

Throughout this book, I will detail broad concepts and dispel erroneous conclusions related to the Law of Attraction. I will unravel a collection of nuances about the process, helping you complete the picture with the missing pieces.

The idea behind this book is to provide you with that "aha" moment; an epiphany that should eliminate any constraints you have toward these practices. Sometimes, there's a need for a slight perspective shift; other times, there's a need to understand the hidden misconceptions or myths that block many from getting the results they want.

For clarity, here are the definitions of the three terms we'll be using to expand on these topics:

- **Myth**: A narrative that is adopted by the masses but represents a false truth or idea.
- **Misconception**: A misunderstanding of an idea based on faulty logic or reasoning.
- **Mistake**: An ineffective approach to a concept or practice.

If this is the first time you are reading any of my books, you'll quickly realize that when I dig into these topics, my intention is to leave no stone unturned. I believe in brutal honesty and know that when people fully understand the core elements of the Law of Attraction, manifesting becomes much easier and the ideas behind it become much clearer.

If you're entirely new to the concept, this book can still serve its purpose, helping you understand principles that, when applied, can move you closer to achieving your goals. We'll touch on a few ideas that I've mentioned in my earlier works; however, we'll outline exactly where there is room for misinterpretation. We will also debunk the biggest myths behind manifesting that prevent people from both utilizing and trusting their own power.

I've been working in this field for many years, and I will be sharing many of the principles I've learned through personal mentors, experience, and self-reflection. There's a lot of information out there, and while some might look nice on paper, the truth of the matter is that if you don't apply the teachings for yourself, you'll never know which ones are more relative to you in your current situation.

My intention with this book is to remove any doubt, to clarify any concept, and to provide you with the necessary tools to refine your understanding. You have the ability to achieve anything you can envision. You have the creative power to alter your current reality and bring about the life that you've always known you were meant for.

Therefore, if you have had the intention, but have fallen short or simply haven't been able to get anything to work, then this book is for you. If you have been able to get some results, but they are nowhere near what you initially wanted, this book is for you. If you're a person who wants to move past knowing about a concept to truly understand it within the core of your being, this book is for you.

I'm excited to take you on this particular journey as I know that when you finish reading the last sentence of this book, you'll be wiser and more capable of manifesting any reality you can imagine. The Law of Attraction works all the time, and the only thing you need to focus on mastering is you and your approach to the principles around it.

If you're reading this right now, it's important you understand that this is a turning point in your life. If you're fully committed to the words on these pages and willing to take a leap of faith, then you'll notice a significant increase in positive momentum in your favor.

Know this: The past will no longer define your future if you're willing to leave it all behind.

"Now the wren has gone to roost
and the sky is turnin' gold
And like the sky my soul is also turnin'
Turnin' from the past, at last and all I've left behind."
—Ray Lamontagne

CHAPTER 1

The Pitfalls of Following Your Joy

Block #1: Chasing comfort and familiarity.

*"We cannot solve our problems with the same thinking
we used when we created them."*
—Albert Einstein

t's probably not the first time that you've read this quote from Albert Einstein, and it certainly won't be the last. The father of modern physics was also a deeply philosophical person and gave much more to humanity than his advanced understanding of physics. Every discovery he made linked back to human patterns and behavior, making quotes like these not only logical, but also relatable to our everyday thoughts and actions.

The quote above provides us with significant insight to how the Law of Attraction works at a fundamental level, specifically relating to our first topic—trying to manifest new circumstances with an old mindset. In other words, wanting things in your life to change without changing things in your life.

The truth is that, at the moment, your manifesting abilities are working just fine. After all, your current reality is a direct result of your ability to manifest. The problem is that the reality you're manifesting is not the one you desire to have. This is potentially the main motivation as to why you're currently holding this book in your hands.

When taking a closer look at the quote and applying it to the Law of Attraction, the problem becomes clear. Many people approach manifesting with the "same thinking" dilemma. That is, they believe they can find the solutions to their problems. The truth is they can, but, as Einstein so aptly put it, not without changing the way they think. One *must think differently* in order to generate a *new* result.

In this first chapter, we will address common misconceptions in manifesting. We're going to be exploring why manifesting from your comfort zone will never allow you to obtain your desired results and why trading your comfort for more freedom is the key for successful manifesting. Further, we will explore why being open to and accepting of change is essential for manifesting. You'll also discover how practicing "self-love" can hold you back from attracting what you want.

Finally, we'll take a look at the ideas of acceptance and tolerance within the context of the Law of Attraction. Though these two concepts might seem similar, they produce wildly different results.

You may be familiar with some of these ideas. However, I encourage you to read these pages as if it's the first time you've been introduced to them. This will frame your mind in such a way that the information sticks and can be assimilated into your being with greater ease.

By redefining your understanding of these concepts, you'll quickly notice a shift in the efficacy of your manifesting.

MISCONCEPTION:
Manifesting is comfortable.

"A ship in harbor is safe, but that's not why ships are built."
—John A. Shedd

One of the most prevalent misconceptions of the Law of Attraction is that all you have to do is simply put your desire out there, and the Universe will take care of the rest. There's no need to think, strategize, or even lift a finger. This misconception leads practitioners to conclude that they will not have to endure any resistance along the way. The Universe, in its infinite wisdom, will apparently somehow figure out a way to arrange the pieces in your life, and, as if by magic, everything you've ever wanted will suddenly appear in your life.

In this frame of mind, you are 'safe' from any responsibility. You are simply a receiver of the gifts of the Universe and are not a participant in the process of creation. By adopting this position, you subject yourself to the whims of your environment, waiting for your manifestations to come to you—attracting from a place of comfort.

It is within this line of thinking that suggests that one can obtain joy solely from a place of comfort. This is where the phrase "follow your joy" gets misconstrued. However, if you've ever achieved a big goal or milestone before, you'll know how much intention, action, and work you needed to get there. Of course, this isn't always the case. Manifesting, in fact, can feel fast and effortless when there's intention, belief, and a release of importance behind the desire. For most people, though, this is uncommon.

Typically, what we want is on the other side of our greatest fears and limitations. Walking past these fears and limitations may create uncomfortable moments that can shift who you are on a fundamental level—your understanding of how reality works—and how you respond to the turmoil. It challenges who you've been up until this moment, giving you the opportunity to *be* from a new frequency.

Now, this might sound like a lot of work or scary to some. However, this doesn't mean you can't find joy during these challenging times—quite the opposite. The critical key to understand here is this: *Comfort is not synonymous to joy.* Joy is limitless. Joy is freedom from limitation. Therefore, to 'follow your joy' is really to take steps towards the thing that makes you feel expansive, creative, and free. You can't experience this in your comfort zone. Here's a quick story to illustrate this point.

Jarred, a business owner, is trying to scale his business. However, in order to scale it, he needs to be willing to invest in testing out different advertisements. Not all of his tests will work. In fact, most won't. All of the money he puts in will most likely feel as though it's money in the trash. The risk and the unknown then develop a level of fear in him, fear of letting go of the money he's worked so hard to earn on something that doesn't guarantee an immediate result. This is the fear most people carry—the fear of the unknown, of failure, or of losing what they have, whether that is finances or status. It's operating from a fear of loss rather than from an enthusiasm to win.

In the beginning, comfort should not be the goal. There's a time and place to experience comfort, security, and consistency, but when you're in the initial stages of a journey, you need to be willing to let go. By letting go, not only are you more open to receiving, but you're also giving yourself a chance to experience joy.

Joy is one of the higher frequencies on the plane of consciousness. It's a state that doesn't require external things to be sustained. It's a present moment state that is generated internally—and this brings us to our first mistake.

MISTAKE: Confusing happiness with joy.

It's the difference between happiness and joy that puts many people on the wrong paths. After all, we are all familiar with the phrase, "in the pursuit of happiness," which is, in a way, the ethos of modern capitalism. The reason this is so important to clarify is because of the nature of many Law of Attraction teachings. We're always looking for more outside of us to fill what we have lacking inside. The pursuit of happiness is a never ending, never present, and never satisfying pursuit. It's what causes people to chase money over service, status over love, and pleasure over fulfillment.

While happiness and joy may seem synonymous, happiness is a subdimension within joy. Happiness is rooted in temporary occurrences. For example, you can be happy that it's sunny outside. You can be happy about your job, car, clothes, or anything external. These are all external elements, the sources of which don't come from within. Happiness is an outward expression. It's a temporary occurrence, not a state of permanence. Happiness can also be linked with pleasure and our tendencies to seek instant gratification.

Joy, on the other hand, relates to your inner world. It allows you to experience the positive side of all moments, whether they are comfortable or uncomfortable. Joy is about falling in love with the process and accepting your current situation for what it is - a part of the journey. Doing this will certainly reduce the weight of discomfort whenever you find yourself in uncomfortable situations. That said, you will not be immune from experiencing these challenging moments.

It's during these challenges that finding glimmers of happiness becomes a difficult task. Therefore, we must turn to developing joy instead. With joy comes meaning and purpose, two aspects that keep you focused on what's truly important. Joy is a unique way of looking at things and of making sense of the world. Joy is a way of positively enduring the hardships on your journey to your ideal reality.

Joy will never come from sitting on the sidelines. It'll only come when you move toward the pursuit of fulfilling your potential, and enjoying every second of it. Only by accepting your fears and walking through those fears, toward your desire, will you be *follow-*

ing your joy. You see, by maintaining the thought of the desire in your mind, yet not pursuing it, you will obtain a temporary sense of 'happiness.' To actually attract joy, you need to be willing to put the desire to the test and turn it into an intention.

As happiness relies on external elements, joy is about understanding that everything, regardless of outcome, is simply a part of the journey. Rejections, failures, and challenges may not feel good at first, and that's okay. Having a willingness to accept change and let go isn't always easy. It's why most people aren't willing to do it. It's also why most people are manifesting the life they *think* they want. They justify small dreams because they don't believe they can have the big ones.

Joy is the result of understanding what matters most in our lives. It's about having an *authentic* life experience and being in alignment with your true nature. Sometimes, following your joy may take you to deep and dark valleys, only to make you appreciate the sunlight and clear sky. It is within these deep and dark valleys you will undergo your most significant internal shifts and changes.

It is critical to understand why and how misconceptions regarding the Law of Attraction have taken root, but it is equally imperative we address how to move past these misconceptions and move into manifesting what we truly deserve.

SOLUTION: Be willing to accept change.

For some people, this idea can be difficult to come to terms with. It's not always fun to roam outside your comfort zone, but when you make it to the other side of the discomfort, you typically will gain valuable reference experience and become wiser. However, the thought of playing the game of life in an area we aren't comfortable, reactivates all of our ancient animal triggers and instincts.

Here's one way of reducing the effects of these triggers. Instead of seeing it as stepping outside of your comfort zone, try to reframe your mind to see it as an *expansion* of your comfort zone. It's not the same as stepping outside of it. It's a more proactive and less reactive intention.

Intention is defined as the resoluteness to have or act. Your expectations won't always be met, but only with intention are you able to manifest your dream reality. Intention is the cornerstone behind every creation. The more intentional you are with your thoughts and actions, the more deliberate you are as a creator.

Begin by taking gradual steps. Think of it this way. Have you ever entered a cold body of water? Most people don't jump in right away; they tend to acclimatize their bodies slowly. Perhaps they only dip their toes into the water to get a feel for it—to prepare their minds for the full body submersion. Once the toes have acclimated, they may splash a bit of water on their legs, arms, and chest, getting used to the feeling of the water until they are ready to take the plunge. Similarly, you'll begin small and build up, ever expanding your zone of comfort.

Expanding your comfort zone will change the way you show up in the world. You'll live less in fear and scarcity and more in confidence and abundance. The less triggered you are by your environment, the more open you will be to taking risks that lead you down the path of your deepest desires.

MISCONCEPTION: All you have to do is ask and it is given.

Throughout the industry of the Law of Attraction, it's often been mentioned that all you need to do is place your order with the Universe and lean back. While some aspects of this is true, such as letting go and having faith, it becomes counterproductive if you do this without any proactive actions to change the way you see your relationship with your desire.

Often, the person you are now is the same person that managed to manifest the life you have today. Aside from the circumstances you were born into, your actions, thoughts, feelings, responses, and decisions have led you to this point in time and space. The reality you manifest is mostly a result of the identity you embody. Of course, there will always be room for unexpected and spontaneous situations to manifest, but in general, your reality is built as a result of the person you are choosing to be, as opposed to the environment itself.

> *"Insanity is doing the same thing over*
> *and over and expecting different results."*
> **—Rita Mae Brown**

This quote applies to many things, but particularly *who* we are choosing to be. Aside from your actions, changing how you see yourself in relation to the world around you is necessary to bring about the change you desire. When you change your perceptions about the type of person you are, it will become easier to sustain the actions, thoughts, and emotions that follow. However, if you keep identifying as a person who is trying to escape or change your life, you will only continue to see circumstances that prove this to be true.

Your external world is a direct reflection of your internal world, meaning the ideas, perspectives, beliefs, thoughts, and emotions all create and sustain the reality that correlates with them. Therefore, being the same person you have always been will only allow you to obtain the same results you have always seen.

For example, let's say you are interested in building a prosperous million-dollar business. The desire is quite clear—you want to achieve success with your business. However, if you harbor a mentality of poverty and lack, or you chase after every new gimmick or idea that presents itself, you'll never be able to achieve this reality. This is because you'll always be engaging in *escapism behavior*, trying to get somewhere as opposed to already feeling you're destined for the place you want to be.

This poverty mindset is a reinforced belief system that incorporates different ideas about wealth and wealth accumulation. For example, within the poverty mindset, you may believe that you are a victim of other people's decisions and choices, or perhaps you have a fear of spending money on non-essentials. You may be obsessed with constantly getting the cheapest deals or gaining free entry into venues, or you may believe you're lucky when you succeed, yet a loser when you fail. You may also feel like you never have enough resources or opportunities available to you.

If some of these beliefs resonate with you, this could be one of the internal blocks stopping you from manifesting your desired reality. If you harbor this mentality, how is it possible to manifest a million-dollar business? Whether consciously or not, you would be looking for reasons to fail instead of reasons to succeed, amplifying the presence of problems and obstacles as opposed to the presence of solutions and pathways.

This is what I mean when I say you must be someone else. You can't sustain a life of abundance with a perspective of yourself that resonates with lack and avoidance of said abundance. Think from a desired future, not from the past. The Law of Attraction isn't broken. It's simply manifesting the reality you believe to be true, a reflection of how you see yourself in relation to your environment and circumstances. Only by becoming more of the person you know you should be—someone who has a wealth mindset—will you be able to manifest a reality of more wealth.

"If you're viewing your life from the same level of mind every single day, anticipating a future based on your past, you are collapsing infinite fields of energy into the same patterns of information called your life."
—Dr. Joe Dispenza

SOLUTION: Live from the end.

How do you start changing who you are into who you are becoming? First, you must let go of your attachment to expectations—those from others and those from yourself. Placing expectations, labels, and definitions on yourself and your life events is solely based on your internal belief system and the conditioning running your thought processes. You must first empty your cup before you can fill it.

The second step toward embodying your desired future self is by being honest with who you are now and who you'd like to be. Get specific about the traits, standards, and behaviors you need to adopt in order to craft the image of yourself that you are seeking. Disregard any voices coming from the outside, and self-reflect by listening to your heart's calling. Being authentic is key—you're not trying to copy someone else. You can model, but do not copy. This description of your desired future self will change as you move along in your journey, but starting somewhere will always be better than starting nowhere. When you can get clear on who you are choosing to be, it becomes easier to embody that version of yourself.

This leads us to the final step, which is becoming aware of your patterns when they happen and consciously choosing a different path when necessary. It's not easy; you're working against a lifetime of programming. However, if you commit to making minor tweaks here and there—actively working toward becoming that desired version of yourself that can sustain the future you desire— it will become easier over time.

As you adapt your behavior, you will create momentum toward your goals. Once momentum becomes sustainable, you will begin to automatically manifest your desires because of who you are, not what you want.

Become vigilant of who you are and what your patterns are, and actively begin transforming them to match your desired future self. Being mindful is key in making the fundamental changes in your life that will manifest the future you can currently see in your mind's eye.

Living from the end - the idea that you live as the person that already has what you want - sounds like a great concept, and it truly is. It's the most powerful form of identity shifting and manifesting out there. Reverse engineering your future self is paramount to accelerated growth and change. However, it can often contradict itself. Does living from the end mean you don't have to work? Do you just pretend you have everything you want? This leads us to the next section.

MISTAKE: Mixing self-love with complacency.

There's a lack of understanding behind the true meaning of self-love. More specifically, there is a distortion between the ideas of compassion and complacency. People associate self-love with warm, fuzzy moments that feel good. We're led to believe that going for a spa treatment or taking a long vacation are hallmarks of self-love.

While taking care of and treating yourself is certainly a part of self-love, expanding your comfort zone to grow into the person you need to become, to achieve the goals you want, is also part of the package. The difference is that one side of the coin is warm, fuzzy and feels good, and the other side tests your limits, pushes you into growth, and is generally *uncomfortable*. The reason why people tend to favor one over the other is because of how they define the terms.

Compassion accepts who you are but strives to create the best version of yourself because *you deserve the best*. Compassion is deliberate in that it identifies a problem and actively seeks out a solution.

It is the perfect balance between being okay with where you are on your journey and choosing to be better than you were yesterday.

Compassion is critical when it comes to being empathetic to where you are now but takes it a step further and pushes you to make the right choices to improve your situation.

Complacency, on the other hand, tolerates things as they are and, over time, begins to cultivate behaviors such as laziness, carelessness, and a disregard for yourself and your life. Complacency holds you back from being critical about your actions and, as a result, continues to manifest the reality you are currently living, or possibly even worsens it.

If you are complacent, you'll tuck tail and run at the first sign of discomfort, seeking comfort as opposed to growth. This is often an unconscious pattern—you do this without knowing you are doing it. When growing up, we tend to adopt many behaviors that reflect our environment and natural animal instincts. As time goes on, these behaviors turn into patterns and automatic reactions. As we venture into adulthood, we're required to revisit these behaviors if we're ever going to transition into becoming conscious creators of our realities, as opposed to products of our human DNA and circumstances.

Complacency is the opposite of self-love. It's the enemy of greatness.

SOLUTION: Become self-compassionate.

The word self-love has taken on many different meanings over time. To avoid any confusion or misinterpretations, I'll be switching to using the word self-compassion. Fortunately, self-compassion can be learned. A study of more than 15,000 compassionate leaders revealed that a regular practice of mindfulness or similar contemplative exercises can make you more compassionate.

Mindfulness makes you more self-aware, meaning you are screening your intentions and actions. You begin to empathize with yourself and others, understanding the origin of a perspective and making the appropriate changes to create different results. In fact, mindfulness is a key component of the Law of Attraction. Mindfulness supports deliberate and constructive decision making.

Additionally, it's important to practice self-compassion during your alone time. Self-compassion is about taking care of your own needs, which includes sleeping, eating, taking breaks, and enjoying time with friends and family, all while pushing yourself to new heights. It's about setting challenges for yourself and embracing the idea that growth is not only uncomfortable but necessary if you seek to live a more fulfilling life.

Critically, self-compassion is about seeking to *improve without judgement*. Take setbacks as learning opportunities and flip the meaning behind circumstances. If the meaning you give to something doesn't support your expansion and growth, it has no benefit or utility. No matter the experiences you've been through, you can always reflect on them with a positive mind. Being late for work could have prevented you from getting into a car crash. Missing a flight could lead you to meeting the love of your life. We never know what life has in store for us. Never underestimate the potential benefits of an initially negative experience. Choose to view reality and life as your supporter, as opposed to an accumulation of obstacles. Making this little shift can make a world of difference.

Accepting and being okay with where you are, without judgement, is the cornerstone to change. However, this idea has been misinterpreted many times, leading us to believe that we should tolerate bad behavior and boundaries that have been crossed.

MISTAKE: Tolerating negative circumstances.

Acceptance is a key component of manifesting your desired reality. If you are not able to accept your current life for what it is, you will operate from a fictionalized mental version of your life and, as a consequence, will be incapable of making the necessary changes to achieve the results you desire. Acceptance is about choosing not to judge reality and working with what you have, while not allowing unexpected circumstances that manifest to stand in the way of you and the way you want to live life.

Tolerance, on the other hand, is the capacity to endure a particular circumstance or external force *without* responding to it, meaning you allow permissible deviations from a specific value or boundary. Tolerating certain circumstances is not synonymous with acceptance. Tolerance keeps you chained to your environment and the influence of others.

Tolerance will lower your standards to fit the mold. You start to dream within the confines of your current reality. In other words, your dreams become limited by your immediate environment. You find excuses why you can't, why it's hard, and why you're lacking; as a result, you find ways to reason with your current situation. It's playing the blame game. Those who tolerate situations also practice complacency.

To tolerate is to lack desire. It's to see your reality as true and unchangeable. There is no empowerment from this space. When you tolerate a situation, you put yourself at the mercy of that situation, as opposed to taking the reins and making the appropriate changes.

SOLUTION: Accept with awareness.

To cultivate more acceptance as opposed to tolerance, there are a couple of things you can actively begin to do. First, you can begin to reframe the perspectives you have about your current life circumstance. When you tolerate situations, it's because you can't see the potential for a way out. You view a situation from a limited mind, making you feel constrained. To overcome this, it's important to embrace the notion that there is *always another way*, even if you can't see it yet. Developing a 'figure it out' mentality has helped many people find light, even in the darkest of situations. If figuring it out is out of your reach, do the best you can to increase the probability of the Universe showing you an open pathway.

Most people are not willing to accept a situation unless they know they can shift from it. Therefore, expand your perspective of the journey by cultivating more faith and, as a result, acceptance. Allowing yourself the space to let the shift take place is crucial. This comes in the form of accepting not just your situation, but also your relationship with that situation. Do not identify or get too attached with it. Remember, you're destined for greater, bigger, and better moments. Relax into this perspective and allow situations to play out as they do. To take it this one step deeper can help you develop a state of neutrality toward all circumstances. Only from this place can you begin to shift the focus to more empowering and productive perspectives of your reality.

True acceptance recognizes areas of improvement and takes actionable steps to remedy any given situation. Do this from a place of knowing and not from doubt. Acceptance means coming into agreement with the situation at hand but not settling with it. Acceptance doesn't seek to justify the situation; it doesn't seek to escape it. Without true acceptance, we'd never commit to making a change. You must acknowledge both your strengths and your weaknesses to begin looking for ways to better approach a specific area of life.

Second, you'll want to follow through on your commitments. Ancient practices establish that your "word is bond," meaning that what you say and what you do need to be congruent. Back in the day, two merchants would make a verbal agreement, which would be as good as any legally binding contract used by businesses today. By following through with your intentions to manifest better life circumstances, you give weight to your words—what you say and what you do become the same thing.

As long as you tolerate your lack of commitment, you will remain a victim. You will make excuses. Acceptance will allow you to take responsibility not only for your words, but also for your actions. To truly accept your circumstances is to live from an empowered state—to live from the end.

C H A P T E R 2 :

Ending Your Internal Battles— The Focus Shifting Process

Block #2: Skipping neutrality and not letting go.

> *"Empty your cup so that it may be filled;*
> *become devoid to gain totality."*
> **—Bruce Lee**

We are told that we need to maintain a positive *attitude* to attract the things we want in our lives; that in order to manifest our desires, we need to *believe* they will. So, how do we shift our minds to the positive when we're neck deep in the negative? How do we believe we are abundant when we have bills piling up and debtors calling us five times a day? How do we claim we are healthy when we look in the mirror and see exhausted, stressed-out versions of ourselves?

The answers to these questions vary wildly depending on who you ask. Some say all you have to do is shift your perspective, which is nice in theory, but there is rarely an explanation as to how one might do such a thing. When our heads are filled with negative thoughts and our bodies with the physiological effect of negative emotions, a simple perspective shift can feel like rolling a boulder up a steep hill. No matter the different meanings and definitions you give to your circumstances, there's still something inside you that doesn't agree, that isn't in alignment with this new perspective.

Constantly telling yourself you feel a certain way when you don't is a form of escapism. Many of those who start applying Law of Attraction techniques tend to go the route of escapism without resolving the underlying issues. They speak out affirmations to a mirror hoping it'll change how they think and feel. They meditate with the intention of *not* thinking or feeling a certain way. The focus is always on *moving away*, rather than *moving toward*.

The issue is not in the techniques themselves. On the contrary, affirmations, visualization, and journaling exercises can be very powerful tools if used correctly. The block is usually found in the transition from negative to positive. As the quote from Bruce Lee states, you need to be willing to empty your cup (let go) before you can fill it (let in). Most people skip the first step, and it's why they experience a lot of resistance.

A perfect example of this is spiritual bypassing. Spiritual bypassing is the tendency to use spiritual ideas and concepts to avoid facing and resolving present life issues. It can include avoiding work because you're not passionate about it, avoiding tough

but necessary conversations because you don't want to be negative, or repressing negative emotions such as anger and sadness because you think you shouldn't feel them. All of these are different expressions of the same behavior.

If you were to force positivity and try to override negative instances, emotions, or experiences, you would fall into the category of the avoidance archetype. The avoidance archetype is nothing more than someone who engages in escapism and denies the reality staring them straight in the face.

Think of shifting your focus as similar to shifting gears in a car without stepping on the clutch. For those who might not be familiar with driving stick, the clutch needs to be engaged in order to shift from one gear to another. The clutch acts as a block that keeps you locked into a specific gear. In order to freely move from one slot to the next, you must first step on the clutch and remove the lock. If you try to force the gears, you'll run into resistance and end up breaking the gearbox.

Denial of one's reality is like trying to switch gears without stepping on the clutch. You're trying to go from one situation to the next without dealing with what it is that is blocking you from achieving your goals. We're always told to focus on the positive, and while there's truth to that, we need to acknowledge and accept the other side of the spectrum as well. Denying one aspect of reality is denying *all aspects of it*. Some people believe that confronting what blocks us is thinking negatively, but this only happens when we dwell. This is where a major misconception comes into play.

During this chapter, we'll take on a few more misconceptions

relating to the central theme of the focus-shifting process. As with the previous chapter, we'll look at some of the major mistakes, as well as the potential solutions to correct them.

"Respect existence or expect resistance."
—Mark Passio

MISTAKE: Positivity without acceptance.

The first idea we'll look at is forced positivity, or as some would call it, toxic positivity. To be completely honest, I don't personally subscribe to the idea that positivity can be toxic. It's akin to saying, "toxic good," which is an oxymoron. Similarly, positivity can't be toxic due to the very nature of the word positive, which means optimistic, admirable, or beneficial. Toxicity can't be beneficial, and therefore, the oxymoronic quality fails to capture the true sentiment of what it wishes to communicate.

As mentioned above, toxic positivity, as others refer to it, is purely and simply a denial of one's own reality. It's pulling the wool over your eyes and hoping everything will just work out. It's an escapist's approach to life and will only continue to exacerbate circumstances that trouble you. Despite this, many people continue to engage in this type of behavior and thinking.

This is due to the misconception that all you need to do is be positive, and things will change. While in spirit this is true, the positivity needs to be genuine. It needs to come from a place of love, and love is all encompassing. It isn't selective.

If you declare positive things, yet internally you frequently give energy to the opposite, very little will change. If you declare positive things, yet internally you judge your current circum-stances, you'll only perpetuate it. One can't manifest what one wants without genuinely having faith in or focus on it. Reality will only reflect back to you what you believe about yourself in relation to your environment. For example, let's say that you experience a series of negative events which has affected your mood. Perhaps you're worried about bills or a big expense that is coming up. Internally, the anxiety and stress start to noticeably affect your mood. While submerged deep within this state of negativity, you may begin to affirm positive statements to yourself, such as, "Everything will work out," "I got this," or "This is all to my benefit."

To be clear, these thoughts and affirmations do signal an attempt to view life in a new and positive manner. However, they do not make much of a difference if you're still attached to what you want to change. When we blindly express positivity, we do so in hopes of igniting a bit of positive feelings in our hearts. Though this is done with the best of intentions, rather than to change our reality, we only exacerbate the issues, causing cognitive dissonance.

Cognitive dissonance (a psychological theory) postulates that people avoid inconsistencies within their own minds. If you hold onto two beliefs that contradict each other, you'll feel a sense of unease. If you change your perspective of an event without letting go of the old perspective you have of it, you'll experience cognitive dissonance. When confronted with valid information that challenges long-held beliefs, cognitive dissonance comes into play, and we adjust our own thoughts, words, or behaviors to try and eliminate this discomfort. It's the moment before a paradigm is shattered.

You can try your best to ignore these limiting beliefs, thoughts, and perspectives, *but you can only ignore aspects of reality that you haven't let enter your circle.* For example, if you've signed a contract to pay off a lease, but you don't have enough money to pay it, shifting your perspective to make the contract disappear won't result in an alternative outcome. The chances of a landlord letting you off the hook is not completely impossible, but it's highly unlikely, especially to the logical and conditioned mind. Because of this, it's difficult to believe in this possibility. If you're already deep in a situation, it's better to navigate it than to ignore it. A better approach to paying off the lease would be to change your perspective on how you're going to get the money to pay it off.

We've grown up to believe strongly in certain aspects and rules of reality. If you pick up a pencil and let it go, gravity will bring it down. No amount of perspective shifting will change that from happening. Although we have the power to change our reality, we're not at the level where we can disrupt a massively held belief such as the law of gravity. There are myths and stories of monks levitating or making objects appear out of thin air, but those are 'once in a blue moon' situations.

Continuing to force positivity into your life only makes you feel worn out and disheartened when you don't see the results you expect. True transformation only comes from the act of transforming into the desired future version of you. It doesn't come from simply saying the things you think your desired self wants to hear.

The very fact that you believe you have a problem and feel the need to affirm it to yourself—so you feel a different way about it—

is exactly what causes you to feel the way you do. Not only that, but it becomes more and more prevalent in your reality because your attention is always on avoiding the problem. This is why you need to empty your cup before you can fill it.

SOLUTION: Neutralize the bad before shifting to the good.

In the introduction to this chapter, we talked about the idea of shifting gears—the need to first step on the clutch to allow free movement to occur. Within an energetic context, the clutch is the mechanism that neutralizes the importance you give to a situation before changing the meaning you put onto it.

When attached to a particular outcome, event, or expectation, the mind and emotions are easily swayed by that outcome. When you are consumed by a negative state, the mind will enter a loop where it actively seeks out supporting evidence to prove and justify the negative state. Negativity begets negativity, and soon, the mind will conjure up more ideas to feel negative about. It will draw your attention like a moth to a flame, almost hypnotizing you with the gravity of the situation.

When you find yourself in these situations, it's best to neutralize and let go before you do anything else. Diminish the importance of the situation, and become unattached to the potential outcomes that come from it. If you've invested a lot of time into a particular situation or thought, becoming unattached can often feel difficult or as though you're giving up. However, the truth of the matter is you actually give space for the situation to unfold in the best way possible, as opposed to trying to force it to happen in the exact way you imagined it. This is what it means to take the path of least resistance. It's to simply let go and let be.

In order to walk this path, the first step will always be to *acknowledge* the situation. Acknowledge that you need to empty your cup. Notice it. Shine a light on it. See your situation and limiting beliefs for what they truly are, without masquerading or sugarcoating them. Observe the situation from a non-biased perspective, from a place of neutrality. At this stage, there are no labels, assumptions, or opinions. Sure, you can give names to help with the description, but to define them as "good" or "bad" is not the purpose of this step. The purpose is to see that this aspect of reality that you are choosing to acknowledge is simply another sector of an infinite Universe. Nothing else.

The second step is to *accept* the situation for what it is—life. To deny a bad situation is to deny life itself, and whether or not you agree with it, every negative thought, feeling, or situation does, and will, exist. This doesn't mean that you must be subjected to these thoughts, feelings, or experiences. You always have the freedom to choose a better perspective and the freedom to reduce the importance you give to any one thought, feeling, or experience.

The most effective way to shift your focus—and your life— is not to invoke more positivity, but to *neutralize* your need to avoid the negativity. Ask yourself questions like, "Why is this so important to me?" and be aware of your own responses. This will allow you the space to disengage from whatever is going on in the moment. If you are at your wits end, and everything seems bleak and desolate, take a step back. Take an objective look at your past and realize that every terrible situation you have ever faced wasn't

the end. Every moment of bad luck and misfortune eventually passed; whatever you are currently going through will also pass, whether you consider it good or bad. You are in constant motion, always changing from one sector of reality to another, in perfect flux. It is only when you give power to the negativity that your perspective and your reality will become stuck in an infinite loop, manifesting exactly what you are trying to resist.

By reducing the importance you place on a particular thought, feeling, or experience, you are able to shift your state to a more resourceful one.

> **TIP:** It helps to create a reminder that everything is always changing, and whatever you are experiencing is temporary. The good times, the bad times—whatever definition you wish to use to describe your life events—will all eventually pass. When you can wholeheartedly accept that you will sometimes experience temporary discomfort, you will be able to stop framing yourself as the victim of the situation or stop identifying with it and begin to look for solutions to increase instances of abundance in your life.

To reduce importance, you merely have to acknowledge that every thought, feeling, and situation has a right to exist. Accept that you are simply a passerby in moments of discomfort. Then, and only then, redirect your focus to finding solutions, and focus on the positives that exist within your control. Yes, it sounds easy on paper. Yes, negativity can be a powerful force to deal with. However, it is absolutely manageable, and it gets easier with time and practice. The more we let go, the more we let in.

MISTAKE: 'Trying' to let go.

This mistake sounds contradictory to what I just outlined, but let me explain. Imagine you're holding a rubber ball with a tight grip. What are the sensations you feel? Tension? Force? When you're holding on tightly, you're exerting a lot of energy to keep it that way. After a while, your arm might start shaking. Your forearms will start getting tired.

Now, imagine the feeling of letting go of the ball, that feeling of release. Sinking backward into your natural state. Without trying. Without effort. Allowing it to happen and not putting any more force on the ball. You're aware that it's still there. It's still in your hand. However, it's no longer draining your energy. This is what it feels like to *let go*.

Most people will *try* to let go. It's like saying they're trying to stay alive. You can't try to go back to your natural state. You *already are* that state. You're just holding on tightly to things that pull you out of it. The shift here is simple. Here's a technique to help.

SOLUTION: Redefine narratives and fall back into awareness.

We're told that in order to live our best lives, we need to live in our dream house, be married to our dream partner, and feel positive all the time. What if all of this was a lie? What if every single assumption you've ever had about reality creation was a lie? Where would you stand?

The reason I'm asking these questions is to get you into an observer state. If you don't take a stand, you don't identify with any particular thought pattern or perspective. You're just observing from the sidelines. It's from this place of observation that all the different potential perspectives will present themselves, and you can begin picking and choosing the one that elevates you the most in terms of how you think and feel about yourself and your reality.

Question your assumption. What is the cause behind you feeling unworthy? What is the cause behind you feeling like you lack abundance? Question it. Think of it from a higher position, from a higher consciousness. What if what you were thinking wasn't true? What if that thought, belief, or perspective was a lie? What if your dream isn't as amazing as you think it is? What if your past didn't happen the way you think it did? You can't let go of thoughts and feeling when you've identified with them. Remove those pieces of your perceived identity, and you'll realize just how easy it is to break down the reasons that keep them alive.

Another misconception around letting go is that it all happens in the mind. This isn't true. Redefining events can certainly help, but it should be followed with a release of emotion. Remember, fall back into your natural state, without identifying with anything. When you don't identify with anything, you're connected to everything. This is your natural state. Infinite. To think otherwise is untrue.

When you sink back into your natural state of awareness, you'll never need to try to let go. It'll happen naturally, just like when you choose your dreams versus fight for them.

MYTH: You should fight for your dreams.

"To appreciate the best opportunity for attack and defense, you must fully understand the rhythm of movement."
—**Sadami Yamada**

I find it only appropriate that we explore a little bit about martial arts in a chapter entitled "Ending Your Internal Battles." When it comes to the Law of Attraction, the practice of Aikido embodies the philosophy in the best way. Aikido is a form of martial arts where you defend yourself without attacking your opponent, simply by using their weight and momentum to redirect the resulting force into empty space, thereby negating the efficacy of the attack.

I frequently run into people who are disciplined, dedicated, and determined to change their lives but don't seem to make any significant headway. As they have told me their stories, I have seen how they battle and rage against their inner demons, using all their might to change their habits and fate. At the end of the day, they usually end up exhausted and without having made any real progress. The reason for this is simple; they rely only on their willpower. Willpower is an internal resource you can access, but it's limited solely to the maximum definition you can assign it. In other words, you become your own limitation, and sometimes there are obstacles that seem bigger than ourselves.

When experiencing internal conflicts, your willpower can sometimes pale in comparison to the issue. For example, you may have a habit of procrastinating that you desperately want to be rid of, but no matter how much you try, you simply can't stop engaging with distractions. This is because you are trying to stop a habit that is deeply rooted inside of you—a part of your identity. The momentum of the habit is a powerful force in your life. If it wasn't, you wouldn't be having a problem with it. Using your willpower against this kind of force is like trying to swim against the current. No matter how much you paddle, the force of the current will always win.

However, when you behave as an Aikido master would, you realize that fighting these urges, triggers, and reactions is pointless and only results in tiring yourself out. However, this doesn't mean that you are doomed to repeat the same mistakes over and over. Rather, Aikido acknowledges the moment you are living in, rather than emphasizing perfection. By trying to use force to change your habits—bits of your personality or identity—you only continue to manifest what you don't want. If you identify as a person who is "trying to change," you'll only ever be that person.

SOLUTION: Let go of the need to struggle.

Just like the Aikido master, you can learn to use the momentum of a situation and redirect it toward something that will diminish the impact. Staying true to the procrastination example from above, you could, instead of desperately trying not to procrastinate, designate certain times of the day for "productive procrastination."

If you know you're not going to do an activity you planned to do and catch yourself procrastinating, instead of feeling guilty about it, *change the nature of your procrastination.* Instead of checking your social media feed, sit back and do nothing for ten minutes. Replace the unproductive activity with the practice of doing nothing. Sit in silence. From this place, you aren't productive, but you're also not unproductive. To practice the act of being present with a thought, feeling, and situation is the starting point to transform it. When you can get comfortable with doing nothing, it's easier to shift your focus to doing what you know you need to do.

The reason we engage in distractions and activities of instant gratification is because of our inability to sit with ourselves. This is why a daily meditation practice is so important. If we always try to escape from our thoughts and feelings, we'll engage in even the most harmful of activities to do so. Let go of this struggle and need to fight.

Sometimes, it's better to focus your efforts on letting go, as opposed to being proactive in your pursuit of a goal. When we let go, we naturally find ourselves in a better position to receive. This is when manifesting becomes quite effortless because clarity is gained, opportunities begin falling in your lap, consistency begins to build, and intuitive hunches start emerging.

Of course, this doesn't mean that you should always be sitting back and letting go. There's a time and place for proactive action too. The point is not to fight the force of your habits, feelings, and situations, but to disengage with them on an energetic level, and redirect the momentum toward activities that produce the highest return. Engage with power, not force. Try your best, *not* your hardest.

In the physical realm, this may look like clearing out your desk, blocking out time to be alone, or choosing a new location

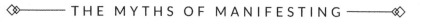

to work from. Knowing what conditions to change in your environment will come when you're no longer focused on avoiding your urges, but rather on redirecting them to an activity that is more productive.

"Man thinks he lives by virtue of the forces he can control, but in fact, he is governed by power from unrevealed sources, power over which he has no control. Because power is effortless, it goes unseen and unsuspected. Force is experienced through the senses; power can be recognized only through inner awareness."
—David R. Hawkins

You may have noticed that there was a central theme running throughout the topics discussed to this point—force. It seems the more we try to force things, the less likely we are to get the results we expect. Perhaps this is because force is about brute physical action, as opposed to tapping into the infinite potential of power.

There's a major difference between power and force. The truth of the matter is that you don't need to be mighty, intimidating, or authoritative to be powerful. For example, confident people don't need to try to make others like them. They naturally exude an energy that makes them attractive. Force is limited by the mind and body. Power, however, taps into an alternate field of energy that is much stronger—the heart. Power transforms.

We must learn to move through life like the Aikido master, guiding the momentum, rather than fighting it. We must redirect the impact negative events have on us and repurpose the energy to propel us to our desires. We do this by facing the conflict in our lives and acknowledging the conflict's right to exist and work them from a place of power. Acceptance, love, allowance, neutrality, nonattachment, emptiness, nonjudgement—these are all avenues to make a shift in focus and, as a result, a shift in your life. Only when you accept what you do not want can you change it. The greatest power you have is the power to choose whether or not to give your power away to a particular situation. In every moment, you have this choice.

Sometimes the forces of life can be overwhelming, especially if you're locked in a period of adverse events. Don't fight it. Don't give it more meaning than you have to. Neutralize yourself in relationship with the event. Let go of your attachment to expectations. Once you've sat in this emptiness, begin shifting your focus to more positive perspectives. This will set you on a path to high-vibrational living.

CHAPTER 3:

The False Narrative around Positivity

Block #3: The chase to feel happy all the time.

"This planet is evolving into a higher vibration of love, generosity, compassion, and contribution. The more you get into sync with that vibration, the more life will see you as a collaborator in its evolution and give you the resources you need to make as big of an impact as you are willing to make."

—Kyle Cease

When it comes to the Law of Attraction, you get the most out of life when you live in higher vibrational states. When you are grateful, positive, abundant in mind and spirit, projecting love and understanding, the sun seems to shine a bit brighter for your day-to-day activities. Not only do you have an intrinsic knowledge of this fact, but virtually every book, video, or seminar on the Law of Attraction reiterates it.

That being said, does higher vibrational living mean that we need to be positive all the time? Is this even possible? The idea that we need to be in a positive state all the time can actually work against our intentions. When we find ourselves in situations where we can't muster up any positive thoughts or emotions, we feel like failures and fakes. We feel like we're going to attract more negative situations because of our negative thoughts and emotions.

In the previous chapter, we talked a lot about forced positivity. This chapter will expand on the *why*. What is driving this perspective? Why do we always want to change, be better, and be more than we already are?

Since the beginning of human tribes and civilizations, there's always been a social hierarchy—a need or desire to be above others and not below them, whether in wealth, status, attraction, physical strength, or even intellect. Modern society continues to be structured around ideas of competition, productivity, and consumerism; if you aren't able to keep up with the latest and greatest trends, you'll be left behind and ostracized. Personal value is often based on the number of zeros you have in your bank account or, within the world of social media, the number of followers you have. Actual success or wisdom isn't even required to become popular or influential nowadays.

The people we see online are filtered projections of the actual person. All their fears, failures, internal struggles, and low points are edited out of the feed, only showing you one version—their best. We see these people being happy and living life to the max and yearn to be as confident, happy, and put together as they are. However, when expectations don't align with where we are, we begin to doubt ourselves, giving into negative thoughts and emotions—justifying it.

As we compare ourselves and find that we aren't always as happy or confident as we should be, we begin to scorn ourselves. As a result, we get caught in a pattern of always trying to improve, be better, and be more than we are, without recognizing that we are enough *now*. There's nothing inherently bad about wanting to improve or change your situation. Everyone should aspire to it if they feel called to. Have a purpose or a goal. However, it should never come at the cost of your self-respect or self-esteem.

In this chapter, we're going to shine a light on negative thoughts and emotions. We'll explore why it's okay to be sad, afraid, unsatisfied, angry, and exist in lower vibrating states. In today's world, perfection is the goal. However, perfection is a bumpy and often infuriating road to unhappiness. This doesn't mean that we should settle for mediocrity. Giving our best in every situation should be the gold standard of our behavior. That being said, getting caught in the web of trying to be perfect or taking every right turn can be a prison of fear.

Perfection makes you second guess yourself, be overly critical of your shortcomings, and can keep you locked in your current reality. Perfection causes you to spend a large portion of your day thinking and contemplating, as opposed to being and creating. Every day we receive information from social media, entertainment, work, emails, podcasts, and more, most of which confirm a standard of beauty, success, value, and happiness determined by others, rather than ourselves. We live our lives comparing ourselves to others, measuring our self-worth based on how much we've accomplished, how strong we are, and a myriad of other definable qualities. It's what makes us human. It's also what drives the majority of us to better our situations. On the other side, it's also what keeps many of us deeply unsatisfied, even when we have everything we could ask for.

It's no wonder we have the tendency to feel as though we're not enough. We're always on a chase, never in the moment.

Throughout the rest of this chapter, we'll explore the impact our external and internal worlds have on our vibration and will also explore how much of our desires are not even our own. We will dive into specific solutions to allow you to detach yourself from the need to always be better or have more, and how doing this will actually attract it all anyway.

MISTAKE: Comparing yourself to others.

"Comparison is the thief of joy."
— Theodore Roosevelt.

It's true that for growth to occur, we must face our shortcomings, accept them, and learn from them in order to make active improvements in our lives. If we simply avoid our shortcomings, we are bound to repeat the same mistakes over and over. Within the context of the Law of Attraction, many people mistakenly think that shortcomings are a result of improper manifestation.

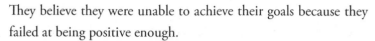

They believe they were unable to achieve their goals because they failed at being positive enough.

As noted earlier, this isn't entirely our fault. Seeing that the world outside of us constantly projects a distorted definition of success, it's no wonder we feel this way. The problem is what we don't see. We don't see these influencers and celebrities experiencing their countless failures and setbacks. We don't see the times they doubted themselves and thought they wouldn't make it. Within the context of our public personas, we don't like to advertise our mistakes and setbacks as this makes us appear to be "less than" to those that surround us.

When we constantly compare ourselves to the seemingly perfect image of others, it is impossible to keep up. We fall prey to projected success which appears to be consistent and nearly instantaneous. Within our own internal thought patterns, we begin to measure ourselves against individuals who seemingly perform at the highest levels of whichever industry they're in. This significantly raises our internal expectations, and when we don't measure up to these supposed definitions of success, we feel the sting of failure. In turn, we begin to punish ourselves, criticize our mistakes, and condemn our past actions. All of this happens because the measuring stick we use is not compatible with the life we've lived.

"If only" becomes our new mantra. We begin to find justifications for our apparent failures by fishing for reasons for why we can't succeed and why we feel less than we are. If you are not careful, this train of thought continues to gain momentum, initiating a cycle of perpetual negativity. Feeling unworthy is the most common representation of this. When you engage in this type of thinking, you begin to second guess all your actions and thoughts, you chastise your supposed lack of progress, and you may even begin to grow envious of others who seemingly have it much easier than you do. When your attention is locked on comparing your mishaps to the success of others, you stop focusing on your own life and your own potential.

You can imagine that people who have such poor views of themselves will have a hard time attracting what they want. If all their attention is focused on comparing their setbacks to other's successes, they leave no space for inspiration to flow. If the phrase, "Where your attention goes, energy flows," is correct, then focusing on the distance between where you are and where you want to be will only increase it. Even if you have a moment of clarity and realize you are being unduly harsh on yourself, a second layer of guilt will likely kick in. You will begin to chastise yourself for not having the right attitude, for giving yourself permission to wallow in more self-pity and self-loathing, and the cycle of negativity will continue.

SOLUTION: Only focus on your path.

Sometimes life is not what you expect it to be. This realization can leave many people feeling like they are owed something. However, the Universe does not operate under these principles. On the contrary, the Universe acts as a mirror that reflects back to you the vibrations that you emit. By wallowing in your own despair, you will only continue to emit a frequency of loss, pain, disillusionment, and dissatisfaction. By becoming a victim of circumstance,

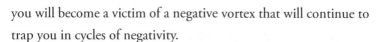

you will become a victim of a negative vortex that will continue to trap you in cycles of negativity.

Instead, accept that you have certain limitations in your life, in this moment, and understand that you may not be able to achieve everything you want just yet. This is a far more effective way to reduce the perceived downsides of a situation.

Accepting your shortcomings and limitations doesn't mean defining yourself by them. You are simply acknowledging that you don't currently possess the ability to take a particular action or achieve a particular goal. You may simply be unaware of the solution in the current moment. This does not mean there are no other ways of achieving your desires. In fact, thinking outside the box can often have a tremendously positive impact on your situation.

There are many people who have physical disabilities who continue to defy expectations because they've managed to think outside of the proverbial box of behavior, and they've tapped into an alternative configuration of how things can be done. Sean Stephenson is a perfect example of this. Born with osteogenesis imperfecta, he didn't grow taller than three feet, had bones so fragile they would fracture if he coughed, and could only get around in a wheelchair. However, he defied all logic and became one of the top hypnotherapists in the world, a best-selling author, and made a great living as a motivational speaker. He accepted his reality but did not allow it to define the potential of his experiences.

Many of our perceived setbacks or failures are artificially created by our excessive need to compare ourselves with others and believe what they have to say about us. People who try to measure themselves against the falsely magnified successes of others create internal expectations that can't be met. One of the primary keys to happiness is to remove your gaze from others and to reorientate it toward yourself. This is difficult to do in a world where the entire planet's population fits in your pocket and is literally a tap or swipe away. However, by becoming more disciplined in your engagement with social media and reducing the hours you dedicate to scrolling the infinite walls, you'll be able to see a measured improvement in your self-esteem, mainly because you'll stop comparing yourself to others. Look to others for inspiration and motivation, not for comparison.

Your life is uniquely yours. There is no one who will ever live as you are in this moment of time and space. Your unique way of looking at life is incredibly rare and special. What you do with this awareness is entirely up to you. There is no one else like you, and there never will be. This is an amazing revelation that has the power to free you from the trap of comparing yourself with or competing with others. Comparison is an activity of the ego. Trying to compete with others is a mentality of lack; the idea that there are only a finite number of resources available to compete for is a myth. The only true 'competition' in your life is between the you from yesterday and the you from today.

When we begin to embrace a mentality of abundance, we come to understand that resources and potentials are infinite, and it is only our ignorance that keeps us from acquiring them. Consider the notion that the world is overpopulated. This belief comes from a place of scarcity. The truth of the matter is, there is no limit to the

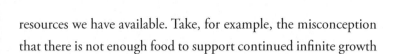

resources we have available. Take, for example, the misconception that there is not enough food to support continued infinite growth on this planet.

According to the United Nations, there are roughly 793 million people starving in the world. This comes out to roughly eleven percent of the entire global population. With figures like these, it's easy to conclude there simply aren't enough resources to go around, and if eleven percent of the world's population is starving, we surely must have a problem with overpopulation, right?

That could be true, except when you look at how much food we throw away each year. You'll quickly realize that the over-population idea falls flat on its face. We throw away one third of all the food we cultivate each year. In 2019, that equated to roughly 931 million tons of food. To put that in perspective, the average person needs roughly four pounds of food a day to survive, or 1,460 pounds in a year. One ton is 2,000 pounds. That means in 2019 alone, we threw away enough food to have given every single starving person on this planet 2,365 pounds of food, enough to feed them comfortably for nearly two years.

The problem is not that we are overpopulated, the problem is the world is suffering from an inability to effectively administer resources. The way we manage our lives is a little bit like this. We limit the potential of the resources we *do* have available to bring us more freedom and abundance. The point is, there is no need to compete. When you begin to shift your awareness away from a mentality of lack and begin to view things from a place of abundance, you'll realize there's plenty for everyone to enjoy. The only question you need to be asking yourself is, "What is it that I truly want?" To answer this, you must look inward and stop looking at others for validation. Your life is uniquely yours, and all the direction you need is already within you. If you're always fighting against your shortcomings and scolding yourself for not moving like everyone else or not being able to perform at some imposed standards set by society, you'll never have the opportunity to discover just how much you have going in your favor.

MYTH: Truth is defined by consensus.

"When you find yourself on the side of the majority, you should pause and reflect."
—**Mark Twain**

There are times when we are on a path filled with optimism, hope, and inspiration, and seemingly out of nowhere, someone comes barging into our reality, splashing their negativity all over our sunshine. If you're not careful, it may rub off on you and spoil your moment of joy.

Can you remember the last time you were in a room when someone who had a bad attitude ruined the energy of the entire gathering? They didn't necessarily need to *do* anything in the form of action; the energy they carried was enough to influence those around them, even if it wasn't their intention. Emotional states are contagious, and whether you like it or not, human beings are social animals. The upside is that the opposite of the example

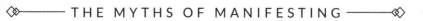

above is also true; a room with relatively low energy can become very lively when a charismatic person enters and begins to interact with everyone present.

While we exist as individuals within a conglomerate, we also behave in a particularly different manner when we come together in groups. Understanding that the emotional states of others can influence our own is something that can directly affect your energy field and change your vibration. When you focus too much of your attention and give too much meaning to negative situations, you concede to the vibration of it. Because of negativity bias, we tend to see the world as a hostile and negative place by default—assuming everyone and everything is out to get us. This is our animal instinct and survival mechanism in action. We expect more negative things to happen because we begin to see proof of it right before our eyes. The key thing to remember is that the origin of the negativity that sparked your survival mechanisms could very possibly have been spillover from another person or situation, not necessarily your true feelings at play. You were not the generator of the negativity, but you were influenced by it.

Sometimes the negativity surrounding us can affect us in such a way that we begin to see the world from the perspectives of others. If a particular group of people sees a situation as tragic or disadvantageous, we tend to adopt these perspectives as the truth, despite the reality that it's merely a biased stance led by the phenomenon of group thinking. This leads us to have more pessimistic, limited, and biased views of ourselves and life in general. Breaking free from these thinking paradigms means disassociating from them entirely.

SOLUTION: Stop rationalizing biased thinking patterns.

How do we disassociate from and avoid getting pulled into "negativity storms" of the people and circumstances around us? Being able to catch yourself being pulled in is a good first step. You might not be able to stop the wave of negativity, but if you can remember to be present and aware during the experience, the outcome of the moment will create a very different result than expected.

One way to stop getting caught in spirals of negativity is choosing not to rationalize everything in accordance with the thinking patterns of society. We have the power to *choose* the perspectives we wish to have and the meanings we wish to place on circumstances. It's these perspectives and meanings that ultimately decide whether or not the tides of a situation will end up working in our favor. We're not doing this in an attempt to change reality. We're doing it to change either the direction it goes or how it affects us.

Rational thinking is not the issue here. The issue is what the rationality supports. Often, it doesn't support our own inner truth, but the conditioned thoughts of others. Allowing biased opinions to cloud your decisions is the surest way to play into the hands of external forces. The only way to find the best path for you is to become an *independent thinker*. When we think independently of the thoughts of those around us, we give room for ourselves to listen to our intuition. We all have access to a deeper sense of *knowing* that can guide us. This is where the heart comes into play.

"The rational mind is a great tool to assess, not to assign."
—Arno Schurmans

Trusting yourself is key. We all have access to an infinite database of information we can call the Universe, the source, the field, or God. This is where insights and ideas come from to help us make the most optimal decisions based on the desires we have and the path we want to walk.

Most of the time and in most situations, we know what we need to do. The reason we often don't trust our intuition is because the truth scares us. It's the unknown, the inconceivable, the thing we would rather not talk about. We know we have to make peace with the relative we haven't talked to in years, or we need to open up to our partner about our insecurities; we know we have to start taking certain actions if we're ever going to grow our business. We know. Trusting ourselves enough to execute it is all there's left to do.

The block lies in waves of thoughts that originate from the rules of society, the opinions of our loved ones, or the judgement of others. When we latch on to these things and let them influence our decisions, we procrastinate on what actually needs to get done in order to move toward where we want to go, simply because it is the easier choice to make.

If you can *drop the importance* you place behind the intrusive thoughts that block progress and can move courageously with faith toward what you know you need to do, then things will begin to change. You will begin to get comfortable in the unknown. Opportunities will start to show up. Circumstances will start to shift. Your belief system will start to reshape as a result of the evidence and proof you witnessed. It all starts when you *stop allowing yourself to get bombarded by the noise outside and*

start listening to the whispers inside. Slowly but surely, with consistent conscious intention, self-reflection, and unattached action, you can make this a reality.

MYTH: You can control reality.

When we say, "I want to change my life," many people assume that we're the ones that will do the changing, that we're the ones that move the pieces around. This is a major misconception. This couldn't be further from what actually happens when life does decide to change. We are not the controllers of reality, but the creators of it. We do not change our lives; we only redirect it by becoming more of who we want to be, and, as a result, our reality begins to reflect it via the Law of Attraction.

When you look at life from this perspective, there will never be a reason to need to change your life. Life is supposed to be exactly how it is. Everything has a right to exist. It is scientifically impossible to change what is (the situation at hand) into what it's not (the situation we want it to be). Both are separate, individual realities. You can only shift from one to the other.

Internal resistance (sadness, frustration, anger, jealousy, envy, impatience, etc.) is built when we feel where we are is not where we should be, that there's something missing. The truth is, you are *exactly* where you need to be. Nowhere else is better.

Now, this doesn't mean we should embrace everything we experience. However, it also doesn't mean we should fight, avoid, or resist it. The key here is to *ignore* what you do not want and *choose* what you do. When we try to avoid negativity, it's because we've allowed it to enter our bubble. We don't need to avoid something that isn't in our energy field. The same applies when we try to control, change, or fight a particular circumstance or situation. We allow these things to enter our energetic space. Any attempt at trying to change 'what is' is equivalent to trying to stay dry in a pool. This will always lead to the opposite of your original intention. First, take a step back out of the pool.

The nature of reality is always to seek balance. Therefore, when we move against this flow, we are only causing more imbalance. Alternatively, when we allow things to exist as they do, it's easier to let them go. When we allow negative situations to be as they are, they often resolve themselves. In the odd situation they do not, the space or insight to truly make an impact will come to you with power, not force.

The only thing we have control over is how we respond to what life presents to us.

SOLUTION: Stop fighting, avoiding, or resisting reality.

One of the hardest lessons everyone must learn at some point in life is this: we are not responsible for how others feel about themselves or others. We are only responsible for how we feel about them and ourselves.

The only control you really have over life is which thoughts you choose to entertain and which actions you are willing to take. Beyond this, you have no control over anything. It's pure folly to think that any thought, emotion, impulse, or situation that arises is under your control. At the end of the day, we are all only responsible for how we respond to the thoughts, emotions, impulses, and situations that come to us. The more consciously we're able to respond, the less of an effect they have on us.

When you truly wrap your mind around this concept, you'll also unbuckle yourself from being influenced by the negativity that surrounds you. Temporary effects are normal. After all, if you're standing in line at the DMV, and the person handling your situation is having a horrible day, the odds of you leaving the place affected by their negativity is quite high. However, when you realize that you don't have to identify with that situation and carry it with you, the effects of it quickly fade away. If something affects you, redefine the meaning you place onto it, and bring yourself back to neutrality.

One way to reduce the impact of external negativity in your life is to imagine that you have an energetic bubble surrounding you at all times. This bubble acts as a barrier to anything that can negatively affect your state, and it filters out anything that won't benefit you.

Exercise: During your meditations, take five to ten minutes to visualize a teardrop-shaped bubble around you. The goal here is to fill this bubble up with as much good, positive energy as you can. Expressing gratitude, embodying your desired future self, reliving past accomplishments, or simply allowing yourself to enjoy the moment can help anchor you in this energy. As you focus in on that feeling, visualize the bubble becoming stronger, denser, and more potent within its function. If you

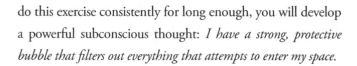

do this exercise consistently for long enough, you will develop a powerful subconscious thought: *I have a strong, protective bubble that filters out everything that attempts to enter my space.*

When people unknowingly try to outsource their negativity to you, it must first pass through this selective bubble before it reaches you, allowing you to choose how you want to interpret the information, as opposed to reacting and falling into the frame of the other person. It's a simple idea and meditation exercise, but over time, it will help you develop a positive filtering system for external forces.

By consciously developing this filtering system, you begin to notice and become more aware of moments when you are the most reactive. Take note of this. What is it that causes you to react? What is it that disturbs your vibration? By reflecting on the situations that trigger disturbance in your bubble, you can optimize the energy of the bubble itself to better prepare you for a similar situation in the future.

The more proactive and conscious you are about how you choose to deal with life circumstances, the better equipped you will become at maintaining composure and poise when surrounded by challenges and chaos. It's not about fighting, avoiding, or resisting what is. It's about developing a system for self-generating higher vibrational ways of either handling or ignoring certain situations. The more consistent you are with this practice, the more often life circumstances will begin going your way.

Whenever you try to fight or avoid something, you give it your energy. It makes no difference the tactic you choose. It simply requires your active participation with it to allow it to remain relevant in your life. Any type of emotional investment into your problems only increases the likelihood of similar situations manifesting in your life.

When you fixate on the problem that screams the loudest, you're trying to fight what you don't want, or you're trying to avoid it. Both of these strategies only serve to keep you tied to the problem you're facing. The best remedy is to stop fixating all of your energy on your problems and instead spend your time working on improving your strengths. This is a form of self-care. It's a form of investing in your own self-worth, which will build up your self-esteem and will ultimately impact your base vibration in a positive way.

When you stop trying to impose your idea of how things ought to be in the world and start to focus in on maximizing your own self-image in relation to it, the problems that you face will fade away with time.

The Light Side Of Negativity

Although we've extensively explored the benefits surrounding positive thinking, the main takeaway of this chapter is to understand that you don't always have to be in a positive state to manifest the life you want. We have a right to feel negative emotions from time to time and to ultimately use them to our benefit, either as a form of guidance or as inspiration to take action.

It is naïve to expect that life will always treat us pleasantly. We all go through growing pains; we all get bumps and bruises—both physically and emotionally—and at some point, our hearts will start to feel the sting. Thinking that we always have to be positive is an inhuman feat. When we try to resist our dark sides, we only make them become more prevalent in our lives. Similarly, by trying to avoid negative situations or the negativity of others, we only increase the importance of it and, as a result, make it more prevalent.

It is vital that you begin to look at your own life as a journey, complete with many short sprints and moments. You are on a path of growth, and growth isn't always linear or pleasant. However, when you begin to cultivate an abundant mindset and view life through the lens of gratitude, even negative situations will become beneficial to you in the long run. This is because you will learn that you are here to grow and evolve. We know that missteps are a part of life, and when we keep our eyes on our intentions, even a perceived failure can work in our favor.

To do this, it will require you to realize just how special you truly are. While your pain and suffering might be uniquely yours, so is your potential and joy. You have a canvas that is ready to be painted on. Don't allow the negativity of the world influence your experience. Set your boundaries and remember to focus on the good while accepting the bad. Life gets fun when we're okay with everything that comes, yet we still have the intention to move toward everything we want.

CHAPTER 4:

The Bad to Worse Cycle

Block #4: Living too much in duality.

"You never know what worse luck your bad luck has saved you from."
—Cormac McCarthy

t's easy to think positive thoughts when you're living your best life, but it becomes infinitely more difficult when the opposite is true. Sometimes, no matter the quality of your intentions or actions, you may find yourself in a bad situation that has nothing to do with the thoughts you think or the emotions you feel.

Deep down, we know that there are spells of fortune. There's evidence of this phenomenon hidden within our language with phrases such as, "Sometimes you're on top, and sometimes you're on the bottom," or, "They ran out of luck." You have observed things magically going your way—you were in the flow of things— and sometimes, no matter how much you try, there is a cloud of bad luck raining on your parade. You might be fighting for your dreams, but for some reason, the dreams fight back.

It wasn't by your choice or your design. The truth of the matter is, life is always in constant oscillation and will never always present you with moments of constant pure bliss. Sometimes, these bouts of unfortunate events can span over days or even weeks. Some people have reported their entire year was terrible. However, when these bad luck spells play out again and again, it could also be an indication of another mechanism at play - negative future projection loops.

This chapter is all about understanding this mechanism and how you can escape the field of influence of these loops in order to get your life back on track.

Bad luck and good luck come and go in your life. While there's nothing you can do to completely avoid bad luck, you can diminish its presence. However, if you get caught in a negative loop, you'll increase the presence of 'bad luck' in your life, and before you know it, you could be spiraling out of control toward worser outcomes.

Fortunately, after reading this chapter, you will understand how to shift yourself into a more resourceful state and fall into a positive loop where instances of good fortune will be more prevalent in your life.

MISTAKE: Projecting a negative future (negative future projection).

What is negative future projection? Here's an example to illustrate it. Let's say you are struggling with money, and while you make

ends meet every month, your margin of error is very small. In other words, any unforeseen expense would upset the very delicate balance you're currently maintaining.

Then, out of the blue, you experience a financial setback. Perhaps a utility bill is twice or three times its usual amount, or your cat is making weird noises when it breathes and requires a trip to the vet, or perhaps someone backed into your car and left you with some serious damage and a nice note saying, "Sorry!"

You can feel the anxiety crawl up from the pit of your stomach and into your throat. Your body begins producing adrenaline and cortisol as your nervous system shifts into its fight or flight mode. Your imagination immediately begins to generate vivid images of how the perfect balance of your finances is breaking. You start imagining yourself being unable to pay the bill, the light company coming to cut your power, and sitting in the dark with only a few candles.

Ironically, if you take a minute to think about, you'll quickly realize your thoughts are a flawless execution of the Law of Attraction, except to your own detriment. You are visualizing while in a heightened emotional state and exerting your energy into the Universe. Because you've allowed yourself to become locked into a negative pattern of thought; associated consequences will begin to appear in your mind's eye.

"If I don't have lights, how am I supposed to work or get up in the morning? If I can't make it to work on time, I'm surely going to get fired, and then what? I'll probably end up on the streets." The mind begins to spin a narrative around the potential negatives, all while projecting a frequency of fear onto the canvas of reality. Since reality does not cater to your desires, but rather shifts in accordance with your frequency and choices of focus, you actually create more instances that match these moments. Therefore, events will begin to change to suit the narrative that you sustain in your mind.

Once your mind is caught on the hook of a negative energy vortex, your unconscious mind will begin to manifest what you don't want, and with every subsequent negative stimulus, you will only continue to spiral deeper into the abyss.

Fortunately, you aren't helpless.

There are ways to shift away from these negative spirals, moving you into positive spirals that send you closer to the reality you want to live in. The mistake most people make is falling victim to a negative attitude when things get bad.

It isn't entirely their fault; we've never been taught how to truly handle bad news. When we were children, we were shielded from the harsh truths of reality; as adults, we do our best to avoid them at all costs. When you find yourself submerged in an undesirable situation, harboring a bad attitude is the worst thing you can do. Even if you believe you are justified in having this bad attitude, it only serves to support the voice of the ego and perpetuates more of what you do not want.

SOLUTION: Embrace non-duality.

A simple way of living an objective and free life is to embrace the concept of non-dual living and sticking to one overarching perspective that serves as a filter for all the others. This is not an easy perspective to adopt for many people. When we frame the world in terms of positive and negative, it's easier for us to fall into an identity. We begin to assign meaning and create narratives for certain acts or situations. A negative situation is perceived as one that goes against your intentions, whereas a positive situation is one that flows with them. While this may seem true on the surface, the truth of the matter is that the labels of positive and negative are simply interpretations that depend on the perspective of the observer.

Picture a young infant playing with some toys. Most people would conclude that this image is light, easy, and positive. However, what if you took three steps closer, only to realize that one of the toy boxes contains deadly spiders, venomous snakes, and other dangerous creatures that could cause serious harm to the child? Suddenly this good scene becomes a bad one. Then, when you take a few more steps, you discover they are merely realistic replicas of dangerous insects and animals designed to teach the child about the wild. Again, we're back in the land of good.

Our perception of any given event creates a meaning for it. There is no such thing as an absolute truth to define any particular situation. Defining an object of focus as being good or bad is a myth that perpetuates across all of society. *Nothing has a built-in meaning.* The moment we recognize that the definition of everything starts at nothing is the moment we can begin to change how we choose to see life, and as a result, change our reality.

If we are able to drop the meaning we give to any given situation, we're able to change the way we perceive it, thus reassigning a fresh and advantageous interpretation, allowing us to respond to and feel differently about it as a consequence. Of course, this is much easier said than done. In most cases, we find ourselves reacting to situations. Reactions are a part of our identity and are automatic. They express themselves without asking for permission. If they aren't consciously created, we simply repeat patterns of the past that create the same life we've always lived.

Recognition that you have parts of yourself that are unconsciously reactive is the first step. The next step is catching yourself right before or right after the act. When you catch yourself in the middle of these emotional storms, you will have an opportunity to interrupt the negative momentum. You can do this by recognizing the moment between the appearance of the situation and the festering of the emotion that comes as a result. Without assigning it as good or bad, you can simply allow the situation to be. Once you have created enough space between you and the specific point of contention, you have the opportunity to reframe and reinterpret the event. This takes practice. It requires you to live in the present moment, conscious and aware. If you float around distracted, it'll be difficult to notice.

Imagine the following: What if the event wasn't happening *to you* but was simply happening? What if this was the best-case scenario, and there were infinitely worse scenarios that could have manifested instead? What if by engaging with that moment in your life, you dodged a major bullet and your course corrected at the right time? This line of questioning is designed to remove you from the role of the victim and recalibrate your self-image in comparison to the problem at hand. Once you have managed to redefine your situation, you then have the opportunity to respond in kind. This means that you disrupt the automatic responses, you stop *reacting*, and you begin *responding*.

Of course, this isn't something that just happens overnight. You need to become aware of your automatic reactions. Journaling is an excellent way to map your mind, thoughts, and life over a period of time. The more aware you are of what makes you tick, the easier it will be to change your response to it. This is why successful businesses track all of their numbers. If there are not enough people booking calls, then it's clear the block is in front-end marketing. If the calendars are booked out, but the closing rate is low, then it's clear the block is in the sales process.

The more we track ourselves, the more aware we will be of our strengths and weaknesses. Most people go based on memory. However, the problem with memory is it's easy to forget things, and memory will be evaluated differently based on how you were feeling in the moment. Journaling solves this by creating a log and timeline of events in chronological order, giving us an objective perspective of our own behavior over time.

Exercise:

Create a journal for the next twenty-one days simply to report and reflect. Whenever you find yourself reacting to a particular situation in a particular manner, take note of the situation, what you were doing, and how you reacted. Ask yourself:

1. When did I react unconsciously today?

2. What was my reaction in emotional terms? Was it anger, sadness, negative self-talk, fear?

3. What or who was the source of the reaction?

4. Why did I choose to react this way? What underlying belief am I holding onto/trying to protect?

5. How will I choose to respond differently to these kinds of situations next time?

While I understand that not everybody wants to journal or has the passion or time to do it, this strategy is meant to help you identify patterns of behavior, thoughts, and triggers in your life. With this knowledge and perspective, you can begin to map out your behaviors in particular scenarios. The more aware and clear you are of your behaviors, the easier it'll be to catch yourself, and the quicker you will be able to readjust to obtain maximum benefit from any given situation.

The End of Negative Momentum: The Advantage Method

There are always two ways to frame any situation—either bringing you closer to your goals or taking you further away. However, the choice of how you perceive any situation will always be up to you. If you are interested in taking a more active approach in shaping your reality, The Advantage Method should be one of the main tools in your arsenal.

With The Advantage Method, you actively frame yourself within the idea that *every possible reality is working to your advantage*. So, how do you do this?

Whenever you catch yourself being unaccepting of a situation, or realizing you don't like how things are going, say a mantra

phrase to remind yourself that you have the power to choose your response. For example, "Wake up! I see myself, and I see reality!" This simple statement tells your unconscious mind to pay attention and to stop following the internal script. After repeating your mantra to yourself, ask yourself, "What is the advantage of this?" and wait until you get an answer. Finally, accept the answer, and follow through with it.

Stop thinking and start following through with whatever answer comes to mind and resonates with your being. You have to feel the answer. If no answer comes, then assume it exists, even if you can't see it yet. Every obstacle is a necessary step you must overcome to bring you closer to your desires. The more you begin to view them as an advantage as opposed to a roadblock, the easier it'll be to overcome them and move forward with your original intentions.

MISCONCEPTION: "Going with the flow."

Many times, when things don't necessarily go the right way, people resort to justifying their feelings and thoughts about a situation by blaming external forces. They outsource the responsibility of their own internal responses to external realities.

If you're at the mercy of external forces, or if it's not your fault, then it's easy to find a reason for your misfortunes. When it's everyone and everything else's fault, there's no need to push yourself beyond your limitations. When you begin to look for external causes to your internal unhappiness and dissatisfaction, then you will begin to notice more reasons that support your declaration.

This is the nature of the Universe. Robert Anton Wilson said it the best: "What the thinker thinks, the prover proves!" When you blame outside forces for your misfortune, you will begin to affirm to the Universe that there are, indeed, forces that stand between you and your desired reality.

Blaming the outside world and limiting yourself based on external forces is just one way you can diffuse responsibility. The ego-self is also partisan to this game. This can be shown with phrases like, "I have a big nose, so I can never have an attractive partner," or, "I didn't do well in school, so I'm not smart enough," or, "I failed at this before, so I'll probably fail again." This is the misconception that negative circumstances will put you at a disadvantage.

While nobody wants to be a victim, per se, being a victim has its perks. You get a lot of attention; people typically try to compensate you for your loss, either economically or through emotional support. You connect with others who also feel like victims. You are no longer responsible for fixing anything. Very little effort and intention is required.

There is a level of comfort in the abandonment of your personal responsibility. It satisfies the ego's need to remain in the familiar. If you've always seen life this way, your ego will always want to continue seeing life this way. Familiar suffering is safer than uncertain freedom.

Other times, this concept is taken to the opposite extreme. People will say they're "going with the flow," when in reality, they are simply being pushed and pulled by external forces without any real intention behind the direction they're headed. You can't go with the flow toward your desire if you do not have intention.

This is like sailing without adjusting the sails. Sure, you'll move from one place to the next, but because you haven't adjusted the sail, you'll go wherever the waves take you. It's a free form way of manifesting, but it lacks focus and clarity. Not only will it take longer to get to where you want to go, but you'll experience more moments of trial and error than are necessary.

Become the captain of your ship.

SOLUTION: Take full ownership of your responses.

The moment you outsource your responsibility, you outsource your power. You remove yourself from the equation, which means that you remove yourself from the ability to instill any real change. You are at the mercy of the other, like a floating paper boat in an infinite ocean, being pushed by the waves.

When you cast yourself as the victim or the floating paper boat, you will be completely disconnected from your main power, the power of choice. You will relinquish your power of choice and 'go with the flow,' letting external forces take charge of the direction your life goes. While we do need to be fluid when we go through life, we aren't supposed to simply allow currents to direct our path. Outsourcing responsibility is a form of detachment, though it is often misconstrued as nonattachment. Detachment is when you release any participation or stop playing the game. Nonattachment is a release of importance or playing the game without being affected by it.

Nonattachment is more akin to a surfer intending to catch and ride a wave. Other waves may pass him by, trying to swoop him up with their momentum, yet the surfer duck dives below the force and allows it to pass. When the surfer spots his perfect wave, he begins to exert a slight bit of effort to position himself to match the momentum, utilizing it to achieve his goal—to surf. Detachment, on the other hand, is akin to a surfer sitting in the sand, watching others take action, and making excuses such as, "The water is too cold," or, "The waves are too big."

This is why it is of paramount importance to be conscious of the responsibility you have for all the choices you make and the direction you take your life in, from choosing what you're eating for lunch to choosing what to say to your client on a call.

MISCONCEPTION: Everything is your responsibility.

The previous section made it seem like everything is your responsibility. If you feel this way, it's simply another expression of victimhood. This is the paradox of being a victim of your responsibilities—you believe that because you have these responsibilities, you aren't allowed to be yourself, enjoy the process, move towards your dreams, and most importantly, let go. On the contrary, you take on external responsibility to cover up the insecurity of letting go.

When we speak about responsibility, we don't just speak about the responsibility of the manifestation of external events, but we also speak about the internal choices of how we choose to see and feel about events and how we act on it. After all, there are people hustling and bustling every day, with many responsibilities, trying to make ends meet. The meaning they tend to place on their responsibilities is that they're 'holding them back.' Others feel pride in being busy, overwhelmed, and on a constant chase, disconnected from the present moment.

Responsibility is about making *good* choices (internally and externally) in the here and now with what you know and have. *It doesn't mean putting more on your plate.* It means consciously making choices that lead to forward movement toward your goals, while at the same time letting go of your attachment to outcomes. Being responsible can also mean saying "no" to people and events that aren't in alignment with your goals. Make choices to see your situation differently and change it, without feeling the need to take or get anything from it, but rather with the intention to have.

Even in situations where you legitimately were a victim, such as a mugging or something of the sort, you have the power to change your behavior in response to that situation. For example, if you were robbed, perhaps you lost a sense of safety and confidence. Instead of remaining the victim in that situation, you can look at it through the Advantage Method and recast yourself.

The manifestation of a negative situation won't always be a result of your thoughts or feelings. Often, it's just a test, a stepping-stone for your evolution. *One thing does not always directly lead to the other.* Pain is inevitable, but suffering is optional, meaning that even though a negative experience might have happened to you, it doesn't mean that it has to define you or that you need to per-manently live in the shadow of that experience. Additionally, there might be situations you can't change. For example, prisoners can't

change the fact that they are imprisoned, but they can change their attitudes toward their imprisonment. This is within their power.

Part of taking ownership of your situation is also being aware of what you have direct influence over in the immediate now. Examples are saying some words of encouragement to a friend or colleague, sending out fifty emails to prospective clients, and introducing yourself to a stranger you'd like to meet. The more focus we give toward using the power we have to instigate change in the here and now, the more likely we are to engage in the things we need to do.

MISCONCEPTION: We're trying to overcome obstacles.

Finally, in order to break out of a negative loop, we will need to reframe how we choose to respond to any given obstacle, challenge, or problem we face. Whenever we find ourselves stuck in a bad situation, it's easy for our minds to get fixated on our problems and supposed lack. We begin to drift into the past when things were "better" or use it to justify the reason we think things are not good enough. We look into the future, fearing what might come, and we begin to unconsciously prep ourselves to play defense. We begin tapping into our survival mechanisms and completely ignore the intention to thrive. This is when we look at reality through the lens of our problems.

As noted earlier, when you place your problems at the very center of your Universe, you increase the importance of them. Giving too much meaning or importance to obstacles will only serve to amplify them more. The reason this happens is because of balancing forces. Balancing forces are responsible for removing any excess potential related to a particular thought. Think about crossing a tight rope. If you were to cross over from one building to the next, the excess fear and importance you give to the situation would overwhelm you and cause you to panic, lose balance, and fall over. On the other hand, if you were just practicing over some cushions, the importance level would be lower, and the panic, fear, and upset wouldn't be present, making it easier to cross the rope.

The same happens with our thoughts in real life. When you place too much meaning or importance on a particular goal, you lose balance with it and push it farther away from you. On the other hand, when you place too much meaning or importance on avoiding or overcoming something, you make it more prevalent in your life.

Remember, when we manifest a particular reality, it's because we energetically resonate with it. When the obstacles you are faced with or the goals you want to achieve feel as if they're too much for you, you energetically bring the desire further away from you or the problem closer to you. This increases the distance between you and the desire. This means that in order to actually move in the direction of your desire, it needs to feel like the normal next step for you. Obstacles become smaller and less influential when we reduce their level of meaning and importance.

While it's easy to logically think differently about a situation, when it comes to managing how we feel, it's a tad bit trickier. When we can learn how to decouple ourselves emotionally from the obstacles and problems we face, it's easier to let these emotions

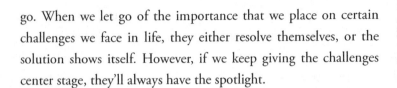

go. When we let go of the importance that we place on certain challenges we face in life, they either resolve themselves, or the solution shows itself. However, if we keep giving the challenges center stage, they'll always have the spotlight.

SOLUTION: Reduce the importance placed on obstacles.

One major misconception that often stops people from moving past obstacles is the meaning they give to them. Obstacles are not roadblocks; they're railroad switches. When we look at obstacles as roadblocks or a big, massive wall that stands in the way of our desires, we tend to fear them, avoid them, or fight them. Obstacles are a normal part of life, but if we're ever to move past them, we need to know what their purpose is and how we can use them to our advantage.

Here's a three-step system to follow:

1. Understand and build the belief that obstacles are mere tests, helping you to have more awareness of your thoughts, feelings, and environment. In other words, obstacles are triggers that expose your internal belief system to yourself and the world. They have to exist, otherwise there would be no way to improve yourself and become the person you need to be. Give your obstacles space and allow them to do be.

2. Reduce the importance of the end goal you're trying to achieve. *Make it seem less than you have it cut out to be.* The more important it is that you achieve a particular goal, the farther away it

will be. Everything you need is in the here and now. Life, in every moment, is perfect as is. If you can begin to see it this way, it will be easier to find the blessings, opportunities, and synchronicities that will lead you to where you intend to go. Of course, there's nothing wrong with wanting better conditions in life, but the results will only start to show when you start to live in appreciation of the abundance that you already have.

3. Ignore obstacles - and I don't mean avoid them or run away from them. I mean *ignore* them, as you would ignore a dog barking at you in the street. If you were to confront the dog, it would bark even louder, but if you ignore it, the dog will, slowly but surely, stop barking. Do not allow it to prey on your energy.

When you make these shifts, you reduce the grandeur of any obstacle you come across. Obstacles serve as an opportunity to guide your momentum in a better direction. Obstacles can teach you about yourself and others, and they can bring clarity to the direction you're heading in.

Make getting what you desire a natural process. Right now, you might be looking at all the obstacles and challenges in your life and thinking how difficult it will be to move past all of it. If you think it's difficult, it certainly will be because that's the meaning you've placed on it. When we release the tension that's involved in goal achievement, everything becomes a whole lot easier.

What if you fail? What if things don't work out? What if it doesn't work? While some people would advise against visualizing your failure, I believe that accepting the possibility of failure allows you to reduce the impact it could potentially have on your state of being.

Imagine what life would be like if the action you took didn't work out? Would it be the end of you and the world? Probably not. Would there still be possibilities to move past that failure, onto greater things? Most likely. Perhaps your setbacks are meant to inspire you to do something else. Perhaps they're meant to show you how to do things differently. The advantage you give yourself is up to you. Be biased toward your own success.

A failed attempt is never truly a failure if it shows you how things *don't* work. When you can accept that, even in the worst of situations, you'll be okay and will realize you have been okay this entire time. Then you can finally let go of the worry, the anxiety, the stress, the pain, and the suffering of enduring a dismal reality, and you'll be able to start working on how you can improve your immediate environment to shift yourself toward your ideal reality, instead of running away from your current one.

C H A P T E R   5 :

How to Manifest More with Less Action

Block #5: Using force instead of power.

"Give me six hours to chop down a tree
and I will spend the first four sharpening the axe."
—Abraham Lincoln

I n today's society, it's common to see many people attempt to use brute force to manifest their goals and desires. They believe that they can achieve what they truly want only through the use of force and effort. It makes sense. After all, everyone who has achieved any sort of success has said that they had to work hard and put a lot of effort into the business, relationship, or life they've built. However, there are those who have put in the hard work, effort, and time, but still haven't built anything truly sustainable.

After all, some of the hardest working individuals in this life have some of the lowest returns.

A humble farmer might work long hours on the field every single day, yet only make enough to get by. On the other hand, there are those who outsource their work and use whatever resources they have to hire someone else do the work *for them*. It's not because they can't do it themselves; it's because their time and energy are better spent elsewhere. This doesn't apply just to money either. In fact, have you ever noticed that the most independent people tend to be the ones most people find attractive? The ones who work the least to impress others actually impress them more.

Discipline and habits do have their place, as well as working long hours. However, when your efforts rely only on this aspect of the equation, frustration and burnout will often be the result. This is why, for some, manifesting can become tiresome, as if it's a constant uphill battle. These people believe that in order to achieve anything, they have to fight for it. At the other extreme are people who believe doing nothing, and simply thinking about their desires, is enough for the Universe to bring them everything they've ever wanted on a silver platter. These people also find themselves not getting what they truly want. This begs the question, is there a balance between the two, a manifesting sweet spot?

The answer is yes, though perhaps not in the way you would think. Fortunately, this entire chapter is dedicated to helping you understand how to manifest *more* with *less* action, as well as to understand the importance of letting go and taking the *right* action to make manifestation feel effortless. We're going to address some

core issues related to your identity and energy, as well as how to escape the trap of Law of Attraction techniques (when used unconsciously). At the end of the chapter, you will understand how to become laser focused with your thoughts and actions to make the most change with the least amount of effort.

MYTH: We get what we want by working hard.

Think back to a time when you worked really hard for something. You spent hours, days, or maybe even weeks, in preparation for a specific moment. You studied everything you needed to study, rehearsed the entire script. You ran drill after drill to nail down the proper form and movement. All of this was for you to get to the moment when it meant the most, and you flopped. Nothing is more discouraging.

While it's true that to affect reality one must act, it isn't necessarily the action that causes the change. In fact, action is merely the consequence of choosing the most convenient and logical option available to you at any given time. Your motivations or intentions guide these actions. However, the one thing that truly gives it the efficacy you expect is *what you believe about yourself in the moment you take the action.*

Many people who attempt to manifest their ideal realities find themselves doing everything in their power to bring their manifestations to fruition, only to get burned out from *too much unnecessary or draining action.* Of course, there is merit in being active and pursuing your objectives; without this dynamic internal drive, you will find yourself subjected to external forces and powers beyond your control. However, action without direction, focus, and substance doesn't achieve much.

> *"If you observe nature at work,*
> *you will see that least effort is expended."*
> **—Deepak Chopra**

When it comes to building relationships of any kind, the same principle applies. Relationships are an exchange of energy. Whether or not this exchange is harmonious is dependent upon many factors, but one of them is if the energy you give comes from a genuine place. Frantic actions are taken only when you don't really believe in the manifestation of your desired outcome. In other words, it is compensation of a poor mindset. An example of this is buying gifts, giving compliments, and people pleasing in an attempt to earn the approval of someone else, as opposed to attracting it by being authentic. You attract by *being*, not by *doing*.

When you try, through pure work and effort, to force your new reality, you are essentially trying to bribe reality with good deeds in order to gain cosmic favors. This belief is something that is instilled in us from a young age: "If you do the hard work and do well in school, things will work out for you!" However, this isn't true in an empirical sense. Does every straight A student become successful and wealthy? Does going to the gym every single day guarantee that you'll have the body of an Olympian? Does working from 6:00 a.m. to 6:00 p.m. guarantee a higher income? The answer is, not always.

Regardless of these facts, people still believe that, through hard, laborious, and draining work, they will be able to achieve their goals every time. Their effort definitely increases their chances, but without considering the forces that are at play beyond their control, they limit the efficacy of those actions. Ignoring this layer of reality can often come at a cost; disheartenment and burnout. The lack of significant progress over a long enough period of time can change their entire perspective of reality, potentially causing them to believe they are their failures, and life is unfair. This perspective manifests more instances that prove it to be true.

Without utilizing your internal guidance system to help you stay on track, you'll, more often than not, act on big challenges that yield little results or give up when the going gets tough. If you want to pursue anything worthwhile, the odds of reality testing your resolve will be quite high. This means that no matter what path you take, you will experience tests, challenges, and obstacles. After understanding this, it's simply a matter of choosing which tests, challenges, and obstacles are *actually worth the work to pass*.

Most of our life decisions derive from who we think we are, based on our environment and our relationship to the activities we engage in. Therefore, our actions, in a way, are a result of our identity, which dictates what we feel we need to maintain it. In this context, *doing* without *being* means you are only treading water. In other words, you exert a lot of energy without going anywhere. Like a fish trying to play catch. The effectiveness of your actions can only be revealed when you know where you are going (desire) and what you are supporting (identity).

SOLUTION: Focus on being.

As we've established, doing without being is a futile exercise, since you expend energy without any particular purpose or focus. It's also the very reason why many people feel that the Law of Attraction doesn't work. They do everything in their power to reach their destinations, but since they don't become the type of people who effortlessly achieve the goals or objectives of their desired realities, they continually slip back into their old patterns, thereby manifesting everything they've always manifested.

Repeatedly asking yourself the question, "Why is this goal, desire, or want important to me?" can help you gain clarity around your core motivations. Taking personality tests to understand your strengths and weaknesses can also guide you toward a more effortless path. Breaking down the illusion of security with your identity can give you more freedom of choice and expression. At the end of the day, knowledge of self is the singular biggest hack to help you make choices that lead to more effortless ways of living. It's never about doing more. It's about being more of who you actually are.

The true process of creation is found by following the BE-DO-HAVE formula—you have to become the person you need to *be*, which will inspire the actions you have to *do*, which ultimately begets the things you wish to *have*. Therefore, one of the most important questions that you should always ask yourself before setting out to achieve any particular goal is, "Who do I need to *become* to achieve this goal?"

When you focus on being the type of person who has what you desire, the act of obtaining your goals will become second nature. A wealthy person or someone who aspires to generate wealth isn't worried as much about the actions they need to take as they are about the person they need to become. For example, instead of focusing on getting clients, a business owner following the BE-DO-HAVE formula will focus their energy on becoming a better salesperson, marketer, or service provider. It's not so much about achieving things that are out there as it is about becoming more of who you need to be. When you have the skills, confidence, and energy of a person who attracts clients, you will naturally start to attract clients. It doesn't come as a result of wanting or wishing upon a higher power to bring them to you, nor does it come as a result of convincing or manipulating them from a place of need or lack.

So, how do you become the person you ought to be today? The first thing you'll need to do is get clear on what you desire. Get clear on your direction. Typically, it'll revolve around money, relationships, and health. Second, identify the type of thoughts, emotions, and actions your ideal self would have. What are they an expert at? What makes them capable? How do they think about a situation? How do they feel about it? What proactive steps do they take when faced with challenges and setbacks? What energy do they bring to the table? What does it feel like to be them?

You have to understand that in this walk of life, you are not stagnant. You are in a constant state of evolution, even though you may not see it. Every day, you choose to become someone different than you were yesterday. Whether you get closer to your future desired self or further away from it is completely up to you. It doesn't come down to the action you take, but rather *how you choose to see yourself*—your self-image.

Naturally, when we see ourselves from the perspective of our desired future self, we notice all the potential we have. A mentor once told me, "You already are everything you want to be" and I like to apply this perspective to the process of changing the self-image. If you can see, feel, and act like that future you, it's because it's already a part of you. It's not something you need to go out there and get. It's just a matter of tapping into that energy internally.

The trick is to define as much of your desired future self in the most real terms you can, then actively work to integrate the mindset, the emotional state, and the actions into your daily life. *Look for proof that it's true whenever you can.* Without proof, the brain will ignore it. When you engage in this type of approach to manifesting, you don't always need to go out and chase your goals; they pull you in.

If you're chasing something, it's because it's running away from you. If you become the type of person who likes to go to the gym and workout—because you choose to identify as a health nut—then the objective is no longer something you chase, but something that pulls you in. The goal becomes a part of who you are. Always focus on *being* first, and the rest will automatically fall in line.

MISTAKE: Depending solely on techniques.

When you journey into the world of personal development and manifesting, it's common to initially focus on the application of

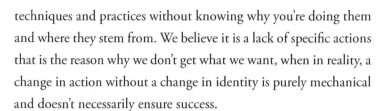
techniques and practices without knowing why you're doing them and where they stem from. We believe it is a lack of specific actions that is the reason why we don't get what we want, when in reality, a change in action without a change in identity is purely mechanical and doesn't necessarily ensure success.

Similarly, becoming a master meditator won't necessarily speed up your ability to manifest the reality you desire. Reading affirmations out loud when your life is crumbling around you might serve as a temporary relief, but this doesn't ensure that you will effectively navigate through it and manage it. Technique is a tool in the hand of a creator. *A tool is void of purpose unless it's wielded by someone who knows what to do with it.*

This is perhaps the very reason why people misinterpret techniques and their relationship with results. If I were to give a hammer to a master carpenter, I could expect the tool to be used to its fullest potential to create objects that are functional, durable, and aesthetically pleasing. This is because the master carpenter understands the purpose of the hammer and the effects it will have on the objects its used on. The hammer doesn't manifest the furniture. It is merely a tool to execute the process. It's the carpenter who decides where to apply, how much to apply, and when to apply the force of the hammer.

Without the tools or the techniques, the carpenter would take a lot longer to build what it is that is being built. That being said, it is not techniques or actions alone that are the sole cause behind a manifestation. It is you, or who you think you are, that is responsible.

SOLUTION: Live a principled life.

Identity is a key factor in manifesting your desired reality. The techniques themselves, the discipline, the work, all are part of the process but they are not the reason why you manifest. Techniques are merely the tools hanging on your spiritual tool belt, helping you to succeed with executing the process. Techniques will always come secondary to principles. Principles are the backbone. They serve as a fundamental truth that creates your chain of reasoning. In other words, they comprise a core guidance system that pushes us to engage with the actions required.

When it comes to principles, techniques are mostly irrelevant. In the case of a carpenter, if the goal is to create a structure that is functional and durable, then one principle could be to use the right tools for the right job, regardless of the circumstance. It's only when the general arc has been established that the carpenter begins to think about the type of tools required to achieve the goal in the quickest, most efficient manner possible. Unless you embody the principles of a true carpenter, the tools will almost never be enough to achieve the vision you have for yourself. It is absolutely essential to embody the principles that inform your actions, so you can achieve your desired reality.

How do you put embodying principles into action? The first step will always be to gain clarity around exactly what you want, then work backward from there. As with any profession or skill, we begin by learning and practicing. You can do this by spending time engaging in the types of activities your version of the carpenter does, reading the material a carpenter would read, hanging out with people who share similar goals, or showing yourself proof

to believe you are becoming the person you need to be. It's by enveloping your focus with confirmations with the *sole intent* of becoming the person you need to be that feeds your belief system and makes you think, feel, and act as if you are already that future version of you. *Give purpose to the techniques and tools you do have.* When you know what you want in life and begin to do whatever you can to become the person that can manifest it, you will begin to inform the rest of your decisions and actions to help you work toward that particular outcome. Below are a few examples of this.

Principle: A clear mind makes better, conscious decisions.
Technique: Meditation.

Principle: We are the average of the five people we spend the most time with.
Technique: Join events or masterminds with like-minded people.

Principle: We first make our habits; then our habits make us.
Technique: Set up external conditions in your life to stimulate you to act.

Does this mean we should simply ignore technique? Of course not! Techniques help us when we don't know what we're doing. The hammer is needed even as an apprentice carpenter because only by practicing can you become proficient with it and know when it does and doesn't apply. Techniques help beginners get into the mindset of what it means to be proactive with their manifesting practices. On top of that, it brings clarity to the process. Without clarity, we often will feel insecure, with a need to control every little aspect of reality.

THE MYTHS OF MANIFESTING

MISCONCEPTION: Control = Creation.

Newtonian physics can be quite deceiving. The fact that we can affect our environment through action makes many people believe they have power over it, as if they're the controllers of reality. Fortunately, this isn't the case.

The illusion of control has many people thinking that if they can build and maintain a certain configuration of reality—everything will go their way. While we do have some degree of control in our lives, we are never fully in control. There are forces at play beyond just our will power.

If you were to objectively look at your life and realize just how little you actually control, you would understand that control is an illusion. In fact, the vast majority of your life is beyond your control and doesn't need you to continue existing or not existing. Challenges, obstacles, surprises, and synchronicities manifest without us having any physical control over them. Your heart doesn't need you to think about beating, the same way your lungs don't need you to think about breathing. Control is a characteristic of the mind. A need from the ego.

If we control so little, how do we create the life we want? The answer doesn't lie in what we can control, but on how we respond to what we can't control. Reality is impossible to control, but we do have control over one thing and one thing only—our responses and choices.

People who try to control every aspect of their lives quickly realize that it's the quickest path to burnout, feeling over-whelmed, and being discouraged. In fear of losing control, we try to hold on tightly to the people and material things in our lives. We want every event, moment, and result to be predictable. This becomes exhausting over time and typically removes your attention from your true objectives, leaving you feeling helpless and, ironically, *out of control.*

SOLUTION: Redirection and faith.

A prism is a 3D geometric figure that has two or more sides of equal size and shape. Any light that reflects on it will bounce out into a certain direction. Depending on how we position the prism, we create different hues within the light, isolating certain frequencies, while amplifying others. We do not control the stream of light, but we do influence the position of the prism to perceive the light from a different angle or form of expression. This is an analogy for reality. We can't control where the light comes from or where it goes, but we can reposition the prism. Reality can't be controlled, but it can be redirected.

When you try to control reality, it's like trying to catch a fish with your hands. This is hardly the most practical way of fishing. It's far more efficient to find the right kind of bait, lay out a net, and attract more fish than your hands can carry.

Why is it important to comprehend that you are not in control? When you understand this concept, it'll be easier to loosen your grip on reality. You can accept that there are things outside of your ability to reason and see. This includes both obstacles and solutions. Your current level of perception often makes it difficult for you to see beyond your current thoughts and beliefs, which is why we want to control every aspect of what we know. We want to stay in the known. However, instead of trying to do everything, there's a much simpler and more effective way to get things done—redirect reality in the direction you want it to go and have *faith* that it will work out.

This is the principle of redirection, and with it comes techniques. However, as with the carpenter scenario, without understanding the principle, no technique will ever work. Redirection is like adjusting the rudder of a sailboat. The boat moves with the wind, regardless of whether or not you put any force into it. The direction and speed of the boat is solely based on the position of the sails and rudder. If you're too busy putting in effort to paddle the boat forward or tilt it from side to side in hopes of moving toward your destination, you'll fail more often than not. In a practical sense, redirection is simply doing what you can with what you have without intending to change the circumstance, but by guiding it in the direction you want it to go. This releases the grip and allows reality to take the path of least resistance.

> *"When you let go of the situation and relax*
> *your controlling grip, you allow the world around you more freedom*
> *and the flow can take its own course."*
> **—Vadim Zealand**

Let go of your expectations of how things should be or how they have to be. Let everything run its course, while at the same time redirecting it in the direction you want it to go. As with traffic control, let the cars move on their own as you lift your baton to guide them safely.

C H A P T E R   6 :

Tiny Visualization Tweaks for Massive Results

Block #6: Visualizing desires for the future instead of the present.

"A human being always acts, feels, and performs in accordance with what he imagines to be true about himself and his environment... For imagination sets the goal 'picture' which our automatic mechanism works on. We act, or fail to act, not because of 'will,' as is so commonly believed, but because of imagination."
—Maxwell Maltz

I f you can see it, you can achieve it. At least, this is what we're told repeatedly at seminars and in most of the basic courses and books on the Law of Attraction. You've got to envision your future—vividly—and create a vision board, so you can see yourself in your ideal house, driving your ideal car, with your ideal partner. You're told that if only you can imagine multiple zeros after that first comma in your bank account, for some supernatural reason money will pour in without you even having to lift a finger. All you have to do is visualize your ideal reality, and you'll reach it.

It sounds too good to be true. But in reality, visualization does work like that, but only when you understand the principles behind it. Many people get inconsistent results with visualization and vision boards. This is because there is a general misunderstanding behind the technique and images. Oftentimes, people will place too much focus on the projected image as opposed to the *energy* behind it.

This chapter will help set things straight and show you what the best approach is to visualization and how you can drastically improve your approach to it.

First, in order to fully appreciate the power of this technique, we must understand that the subconscious mind can't tell the difference between what is real and what isn't. In other words, the subconscious mind doesn't have a filter for what it experiences. When emotions and senses are involved, the impact of an experience increases. Thus, when you visualize, the subconscious mind interprets it as if it is happening right now.

This phenomenon was best captured in a study in which researchers used transcranial magnetic stimulation (TMS) to map out key areas of the brains of the participants in the study. The subjects were instructed to play a sequence of piano notes for five days straight while they had their brain activity monitored. After five days, they were asked to *imagine* playing the notes in their minds. To the amazement of the researchers, the brain activity peaked at almost the same intensity as when they physically played the piano. The receptivity of the subconscious mind makes visualization a powerful technique, even when it's simply an internalized image we hold in our heads.

Why is this important?

Throughout the rest of this chapter, we'll explore how this relates to your visualization shortcomings and how you can make some minor tweaks to significantly increase the impact of your visualization practice.

MISTAKE: Visualizing desires in the future.

We are told that if we envision our future in as much detail as possible, we'll be able to attract it. This is because of our subconscious mind's inability to distinguish between imagination and reality. When you envision yourself in an ideal future, you create the space for such a reality to exist. You begin to shift your awareness, attention, and focus onto a situation that appeals to you. Unconsciously, you begin to shift your identity and behavior in order to bring the image to fruition. This is the underlying and simplest way of explaining the Law of Attraction. However, there is something that most people miss when engaging with this truth.

When you keep the future in the future, your subconscious mind will accept that your dreams will come true *in the future*— in other words, not right now. Most people dream of their ideal house, their ideal career, and their ideal lives somewhere in the future, separated far from their current reality. As a result, they never seem to get their desires to manifest in their present lives and are always only "on the brink" of having it.

Your mind is like a genie. Unlike the genie from the movie *Aladdin*, most genies or djinns are known more as tricksters. They grant you wishes but always with a caveat or twist. For example, if you wished to be famous, the genie would grant your wish and you would become famous, but it would only happen after your death. When we envision our lives in the future, our subconscious minds accept the wishes we have and go on to maintain our desires in the future. Therefore, it will always feel like there is distance between where you are and where you want to be. This doesn't mean that the Universe or your subconscious mind conspires against your good fortune; rather, you have not entirely understood how to effectively communicate your desire.

It's the conscious layers of your mind that are responsible for those subtle shifts in focus and perspective. The issue is one of miscommunication. If you are incapable of clearly communicating your conscious heart's desire, you can't expect the subconscious mind to work in your favor. This is why envisioning the future is a trap. It creates an energetic separation between you and your ideal state of being or way of living, in all dimensions (mental, emotional, and physical), that moves you toward your desires.

Tomorrow will never come. Now is the only moment that exists, and it is ever fleeting. As long as you maintain your future in the future, you'll never be able to experience it in the present. As long as you feel as though there is a giant gap between your ideal state and your current state, that giant gap will continue to remain.

If you always visualize a desire from a distance, separate from you, that's where it'll stay. If it never feels as though you already have your desire, you'll never be the person who attracts it. Now let's take a look at how to reframe this.

SOLUTION: Live right now from the future.

In the previous chapter, we outlined how to become the version of you who would naturally achieve and manifest your goals. This is future projection, bringing clarity to your ideal future self to help influence your decisions and actions right now. In this same vein of thinking, you can understand that your visualizations should also behave in a similar fashion. We know that if we visualize our success in the future, we will only ever experience success in the future.

Therefore, it is imperative that you reframe your visualization from something out there, in the distance, a long time away, to something you are living and experiencing right now. This, of course, is where it can get tricky. How can I live right now, from the future, when my present doesn't reflect the environment of my ideal reality? How can you feel like a successful business owner if you're still working a nine-to-five job?

One way to do this is to bring more realism and attention to your imagination. In other words, define what you imagine in your mind as an actual, real experience. Everything that is absorbed by our subconscious mind is a result of our perception of our experiences. When we can reframe the meaning we place on the experience of our imagination, we can change the way it influences how we think, feel, and act, through the subconscious mind. The more real you can make the experience, the more information you can adopt.

The first step to make your visualization feel more real is to get clear about what it would mean to be that future version of you from every different perspective you can imagine. We have already established this earlier—that the subconscious mind can't tell the difference between the imaginary and the real—therefore, when you spend time as this imaginary self who is living your best life through visualization, you will begin to decipher who that person is—what they are like, how they think, feel, and act, what kind of energy they carry with them, how they relate to their environment, and what they have. The clearer you are in knowing what it's like to be this version of you, the closer you will get to actually embodying it.

The person you are imagining isn't the person you are now because in this future version of you, you have solved all your major problems and have achieved your idealized level of success. This means the future version of you has learned lessons, moved past obstacles, endured hardships, and ultimately been freed from the chains of their mind. The way your future self thinks would be different than how you think now. Your future self would be wiser, facing your obstacles with confidence and faith. This version would *have* the habits and discipline needed to follow through on the actions required to achieve your goals and objectives.

This brings me to the idea of channeling the *having frequency*. Channel the feelings that come from having what you want, and project that energy out into the world through creation and action. In business terms, this would be called shifting from being a consumer to being a producer.

The biggest block that stops many people from taking risks and investing in and trusting themselves is the uncertainty of whether or not the direction they are headed will produce the results they are expecting. However, when you channel the having frequency, these worries, fears, and anxieties dissipate because you no longer create from a place of lack or your attachment to outcomes, but rather from one of abundance — the place of already *having* what you want. Thus, you navigate your challenges and obstacles with a lighter energy (reduced importance), almost as if the manifestation of the desire feels inevitable.

When you visualize your future—in the ideal house, driving the cars you desire, with the partner of your dreams—you might not be able to physically embody the external things, but you do know how to embody your self-image. Therefore, the more you can relate to and connect with your future self, the easier it will be to see yourself as that person *now*. This is why it's so important to get clear on *who your future self is* and truly make that version of you come alive today.

Imagine what this future version of you would do in your current situation, with your current resources. Imagine this successful, resourceful, persistent, and confident image of yourself having to solve all of your current problems. What would they do differently, knowing they'd eventually get to where they want to be? When you can tap into this frequency in your daily life, you begin to harvest the internal image of the person who can manifest the life of their dreams. *Align your thinking, feeling, and doing to reflect the being of your future self.* The more you can become this version, the quicker you'll notice the world around you shift as you let go of who you used to be and become the version of yourself who can manifest and sustain the reality you've always dreamed of.

MISCONCEPTION: All visualizations work the same way.

Everyone's visualizations take on a different form. Your dreams are your dreams. Don't lower your standards or change them based on the approach of others. Stick to your dream because it's your truth. If your dreams do not scare you, they're not big enough. Embrace this fear. We don't get to pick our dreams; they come inherent in us. To go against this is to go against the nature of the Universe. You are here to carry out that vision.

With that being said, there are different ways of visualizing your dreams to give them that extra edge and make them feel more real, alive, and connected to you than you've ever felt before. It's a minor tweak that will dramatically increase the effectiveness of your visualizations. By and large, people tend to visualize their future as an image, a painting, or a movie—in other words, a 2D projection on a flat surface from a third-person perspective. When they visualize, they are not immersed in the visualization as much as they observe it from afar. They see themselves in a scene, acting it out, and engaging with this projection, almost as if they were a fan watching themselves on a movie screen.

Many people with the most beautiful vision boards find themselves incapable of achieving their desired realities. It's almost as if they are stuck observing their idealized life, yet they never participate. They see their dream car every time they get on the freeway. They're always getting advertisements for their dream house. All these synchronicities are happening, yet nothing changes. The subconscious mind manifests exactly what we project, and when you see yourself in third person, you are not participating in the activity.

While vision boards are not inherently bad for manifesting—they can be used as a starting point or means of tapping into the *feelings* of those images—many people get lost in the imagery and remain an observer of their lives, as opposed to active creators.

SOLUTION: Multi-sensory first-person visualization.

When applying the practice of visualization, most people imagine all the external and visual aspects of what they want. If you desire to manifest a brand new sports car, you might imagine what it looks like from the outside. If you're creative enough, you may even imagine it parked in front of your home.

This is the most basic form of visualization. Although it can spark a small level of inner excitement, inspiration, and impulse, it will rarely feel like the real thing. In order to get to the stage when our visualizations truly change the way we think, feel, and act on a more impactful level, we need to learn how to utilize our imaginations to the maximum of our capabilities. This involves two things: shifting your perspective and involving your senses.

The first, shifting from having the outsider (third-person perspective) to having the insider (first-person perspective), means you'll want to slide your position from being the observer to being the active participant. Visualizing from a deeper position of the reality you want to live will allow you to tap into states that you otherwise wouldn't if you simply imagined it from far away. In relation to that brand new sports car, imagine yourself not just looking at it, but sitting inside of it as well, driving it and actually experiencing the car as if it was in your possession right now. Movement of the parts is key.

When you do this, notice how your posture changes and how you breathe differently. Using first-person perspective—engaging in the movement of it all—causes physical responses. Completely connect to the sensations in your body, the types of thoughts going through your mind, and how you're feeling. Play off the image that your future desired self has of yourself.

The more you practice, the more you will know what it feels like to have the freedom of wealth, the love of a partner, and the confidence of wholeness as you tap into this frequency.

This brings us to the next step: involving your other senses. Contrary to the name, visualization can also involve your other senses—hearing, touching, tasting, and smelling. Imagine the new car smell, the texture of the leather seats, and the roaring of the engine. These are all elements that enhance the reality of your visualizations.

For some people, visualizing a scene can be difficult, so they only see glimpses of the scene or experience momentary feelings associated with their desired outcomes. It's good to take time to make the scenery as detailed and as real as possible. Sticking with

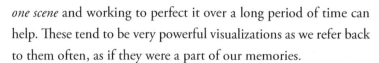

one scene and working to perfect it over a long period of time can help. These tend to be very powerful visualizations as we refer back to them often, as if they were a part of our memories.

Constructing this scene might take time; there is no rush to achieve it the first time. It requires some patience to strengthen the reality of the scene. It's best to slowly build a detailed mental experience, rather than trying to quickly conjure up a moment of success you can't relate to. You want to know your success intimately and be familiar with every nook and cranny of what it feels like to be the person living it.

Because visualization tends to be perceived as a purely mental exercise, it's often ranked low when it comes to its effectiveness as a manifesting technique. However, when we involve our emotions, the practice becomes exponentially more impactful. It's the difference between engaging with the brain and engaging with the heart. Emotions, feelings, physical sensations, posture, energy—all of these metrics allow you to connect with this future version of yourself. Just as you took your time to build up a detailed image of your future self, you should also spend quality time getting to know your future self from the first-person perspective. The more you practice this kind of visualization, the easier it will be to embody it in your mind, body, spirit and, eventually, in life.

This is what high-achieving basketball players like Michael Jordan and Kobe Bryant did to help create more success in their careers. Bryant used to dribble an imaginary ball, going through drills over and over again, constantly training even when his physical body was not exerting any effort. He would tap into the idealized future version of himself and play "as him" in his optimal state.

Similarly, Jordan would envision himself making the winning shot before games to prepare his mind to behave accordingly and find those opportunities.

When you participate in your visualizations as opposed to viewing them from far away, it's easier to tap into the frequency of your desired future self. You begin to embody that future self, and because the subconscious mind is incapable of telling the difference between this embodiment and the current you, it becomes more real every time you engage with it. The more you become this future self, the more the brain will begin to rewire itself to prove this version true. If you think wealthy, behave wealthy, and respond to situations like a wealthy person would, the subconscious mind will begin to look for evidence to support the premise that you are wealthy, making you more prone to make decisions that lead to more wealth.

Therefore, by simply becoming one with your visualizations—participating instead of observing—you will see dramatic results, not just externally, but also in the way you experience life.

MISTAKE: Visualize only during meditation time.

The final piece of the puzzle comes not from what you do when you visualize, but rather what you do when you are done. While it's a good practice to visualize your future every morning during your daily meditation practice, many people believe their visualizations end when their meditation timer runs out. They experience their future self, they walk through their dream reality, and the moment

they hear the alarm bells ring, they open their eyes and continue on with their day as the same old self with the same old patterns.

Not only do people stop visualizing, but they slide back into their everyday behaviors. Everything they experienced within their deep meditative state remains in the ethereal, an experience that can only be achieved when in a deep, meditative state. They believe that when they tap into this feeling or frequency, they are all set and don't have to worry about the rest of their day, assuming everything beyond that point will happen automatically. Alas, they often *forget* most of what they experienced during their visualizations.

Even with the future self comfortably tucked away in the back of their heads, they resort back to *what they know* when conflict arises. They return to the old script and replay the same old reactions to the same old problems they have been struggling with. Don't get me wrong, if you do ten to thirty minutes of visualization and meditation per day, you will most certainly begin to experience benefits. However, if you lock your visualizations within this time frame and do not allow them to integrate and spill over into your everyday life, you'll always be left fighting a war between two selves, both aiming to occupy the same space.

In other words, the self you are now and the self you'd like to be end up in conflict because you keep your future desired self-confined to a designated time and space within your reality. Keeping your visualizations separate from the rest of your life means they haven't become your core response protocol. You are still not fully embodying your future self. You are still projecting an image that doesn't reflect who you'd like to be. This serves only to create more energetic distance between you and your desired state of being.

Yes, designating transformation only to a small section of your day can, in fact, propel many people forward, especially if they're consistent with the practice. However, imagine consciously carrying this energy throughout the day with all your choices, interactions, and decisions. Not only would the changes be instantly more noticeable, but the practice would become much more effective.

SOLUTION: Live through your visualizations.

In order to shift to the energy of your desired future self, you need to release control of who you think you are. Every version of you, both desired and undesired, is a small piece of your multidimensional nature. Therefore, there's nothing wrong with who you are now, nor should you aim to be different than how you've been. When you aim for something, you're separate from it. It should be with you, here and now. However, most people would agree that if who you are now is not manifesting the life you want, something needs to change, and it has nothing to do with what happens outside of you.

Allow yourself to *be* first, accepting the presence of, then letting go of, your current patterns as it is the path to embodying a new you—not just during your visualizations, but in every aspect of your life experience. The trick is to consciously integrate the new thoughts, feelings, and actions experienced during your visualizations, and make them become a part of who you are throughout your day. All of this is to feed your subconscious mind with more reasons to believe that you are becoming and being the version of you that is in alignment with what you want.

While this may seem abstract in practice, the truth of the matter is that there are practical ways we can solidify the habit of being our future self in our present reality. One of the easiest ways is to visualize yourself going about your current routine in the same way the future version of you would. When you visualize yourself going about your day in that future state, you will begin to identify circumstances that trigger the emergence of old patterns and reactions. You will begin to actually notice the disconnect between the reaction that comes up and the state you are currently in. Journaling these moments and triggers will help you catch them and readjust your responses.

The idea is to connect to the thoughts, feelings, and actions of your future self, and bring that connection into your current reality, so you can live as this future self would if it were faced with your current circumstances.

Next, you'll want to see your visualizations as a *memory* that you can tap into, as opposed to an imaginary fantasy land you escape to every time you meditate. This is how you get the most out of your visualizations. Take your time, truly connect with every aspect of this reality, and internalize it. Once you are able to tap into this base frequency, circumstances will begin to shift, and you'll naturally begin to take the actions that bring you closer to your goals.

Visualization is a concept that has a lot of hidden nuances since it's experienced differently by each person. Sometimes, this can lead to inefficient and ineffective modes of practicing it. It's not always easy to be able to envision the future version of you, especially if you are clouded with the problems of your current circumstances. However, if you begin to implement the techniques covered in this chapter, you'll begin to notice a shift inside of you. No longer will the external elements inform your narrative, but the embodied version of your idealized life will begin to take greater control of your thoughts, behaviors, and your luck. Your imagined life will feel more real than your 'real' life.

The subconscious mind has the ability to operate outside of the realm of logic and linearity. It can tap into insight beyond our understanding, and once you begin to communicate with it properly, you will begin to see amazing changes happen in your life.

This brings us to the last myth we'll cover—perhaps the biggest myth of all when it comes to the Law of Attraction. Master the next lesson, and you'll maximize everything we've talked about up until this point.

CHAPTER 7:

Debunking the Biggest Law of Attraction Myth

Block #7: Depending on a burning hot desire.

"Do not spoil what you have by desiring what you have not; remember that what you now have was once among the things you only hoped for."
— Epicurus

Desire can be a tricky thing. For one, it is essential within the formula of the Law of Attraction in that without desire, there is no intention. This means that there is nothing to actually create to contribute to the infinite expansion of the Universe, which is why understanding the fundamental nature of desire is so important. If you fail to properly align your desire, or you place too much importance on the desire, it can feel like what you want doesn't want you.

In this chapter, we're going to peel back the layers of desire to reveal just how people misinterpret this concept and how this negatively affects their ability to manifest their own desires. I personally find this to be the biggest block in Law of Attraction teachings. It's believed that if you want something bad enough, you will be able to get it. It is almost a mantra that is repeated by virtually every personal development coach, guru, book, or seminar, and like many things we have discussed in this book thus far, it is both true and misunderstood. It is true when you become laser focused on a specific task or objective; the subconscious mind begins to work in ways that operate above your conscious understanding, moving you in the direction of the reality you choose to experience. In the previous chapter, we dove deep into this topic and how the subconscious mind operates. Therefore, it makes sense that when you have a burning hot desire for something, motivating you to push you forward, you'll eventually get it, right?

In fact, this is where the initial problem lies and where I find many people take their first step with the wrong foot.

MYTH: If you want it bad enough, you can have it.

What is it you truly want in life? Are you looking for more money? Love? Health? What would you be doing if you had no obligations and no limitations? Most of us have some idea of what we want in life or where we want to get to. For some of us, the intensity of the desire is so great we begin to obsessively fixate on this ideal reality. Within common teachings of the Law of Attraction, this

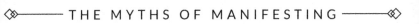

kind of behavior will attract the reality we desire. However, there is a hidden element of desire that most people never consider, and this is what stops many from manifesting it.

A desire, by definition, is an affirmation of lack. If you already had what you wanted, there would be no desire. A desire always comes from a place of not having, which, in turn, creates disharmony between how you view yourself in relationship to your environment. The discomfort of not having creates the initial impulse to set intentions and move toward a place that is perceived to be better than the current circumstances. This is where desire is beneficial, getting us moving and proactive in the pursuit of our goals and objectives. However, *when there is an unnatural amount of importance or emphasis placed on the desire, it compounds the affirmation of lack, intensifying our focus on the reality we are currently in.*

Since we can't teleport into the future to live our desired reality, we are forced to face the reality we are currently in. The more we emphasize this gap between the desired and current reality, the more distance we create between them. Moreover, when you adopt an "at all costs" attitude, it can indeed move you closer to your desires, but at what cost? You begin to sacrifice your own well-being or the well-being of others in order to fulfill this desire. You take shortcuts that are unsustainable and short-lived. While in the short term, such an intense level of dedication toward achieving your goals could deliver some decent results, this kind of strategy will inevitably only serve to deplete you and strip you of any fulfillment you could get from accomplishing the goal. This is when people experience burnout, stress, and overwhelm. What is the point of gaining the world if you lose your soul in the process?

As we've previously discussed, the more we affirm our desire from a place of lack, the more it feels like we do not have it. Hence, our focus and attention are shifted to what we do not want, leading us to focus on fixing problems instead of creating solutions. When you begin to place an unnatural emphasis on your desires, you will fall victim to justifying and reinforcing negative behaviors. For example, being bossy might work to get quick results in certain situations, but it will come at the expense of people's perceptions of you. Perhaps you will justify this behavior because when it comes to climbing the corporate ladder, you have to embody a particular attitude or behavioral pattern in order to remain competitive. This kind of justification can only be achieved when you place so much importance on your goal that everyone else and everything else, including yourself, comes second.

SOLUTION: Stop wanting and start choosing.

When you are fixated on a particular outcome, anything that deviates from your expected script will generate a negative feeling. Most people would call it resistance. In reality, this resistance isn't resistance at all, but a shift to an alternative (and often simpler) path to achieve your desired outcome. However, unless you are willing to deviate from your original script, you'll never find out.

Regardless, you will not even be able to contemplate this as a possibility if you are obsessively attached to a particular path or outcome. Therefore, it's important that you reduce the importance of the desire in order to give yourself the flexibility to adapt to your intentions and circumstances accordingly. Maybe, you'll even decide to change your desire as you get closer to the one you initially thought you had. The fact of the matter is that reality will always take the path of least resistance to deliver to you what you truly want, even if that means it needs to disrupt a behavioral pattern or make you uncomfortable.

For example, if you have the desire to build a business, the path of least resistance might be to get rejected by multiple clients in the beginning. This causes you to reflect and reevaluate your entire approach with how you present offers and answer calls. At first, it might look like the path of most resistance, but if you have goals to grow something big and sustainable, then it's actually the best path. Remember, setbacks and failed attempts are not manifested in an attempt to make you give up. They're actually leverages, pointing you in the direction of the best lesson you can learn to get to where you want to go. Unfortunately, many don't see it that way. They'd much rather stick to the idea of getting clients and making money. Anything opposing to this will become another reason to support their limitations. Therefore, be open to new avenues.

The more attached you are to your desires, the more resistance and separation you're going to feel. Your soul is craving the unknown, the adventure, and the expansion, but your mind is still hung up on one set way of doing things because of the past or fears of the future. To shift away from this conundrum, start *choosing* the life you want. Desire is passive; choosing is proactive.

Desire, at optimal levels, should act as a means toward intention. You want something, set an intention, choose to have it, and begin working toward it. If a particular desire becomes too important and too necessary, you destabilize your energy in relation to it. This can manifest in the form of fear, overwhelm, and disbelief. Contrary to what many might think, reducing the importance of your desires works in your favor. This is how you close the gap between being who you are now and being the version of you that has the life you want. Does the version of you that has everything you want spend all day yearning for it? They don't. So, why should you?

None of this is to say you should dream small or that you shouldn't have a dream at all. Rather, it is a reminder that dreams are just dreams. They're a part of who you already are. There is no need to think, feel, and act like it's this far away wonderland you can't connect with *right now*.

There are three major benefits of reducing the importance of your desires:

1. You become more process oriented. Desire itself doesn't move the needle; intention does. When all your time and energy is spent daydreaming, where is the time and energy for creating? Wishing and wanting is the first step, everything after that is meant to close the energetic gap between you and the desire.

2. You stop justifying negative behaviors. When a particular outcome is no longer your end-all be-all, you will no longer need to force situations to go your way. Negative behaviors, such as getting angry at others, physically punishing yourself, taking shortcuts, or toxic manipulation, are a result of unstable footing in who you are. Initially, you can take this route if the paradigm you're currently in is that of apathy, procrastination, or lack of motivation. However, it should only serve to kick-

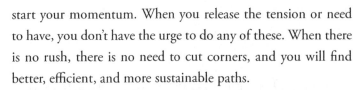

start your momentum. When you release the tension or need to have, you don't have the urge to do any of these. When there is no rush, there is no need to cut corners, and you will find better, efficient, and more sustainable paths.

3. You regain freedom of choice. When importance levels are high, it's a result of attachments. When you're attached to a certain path, goal, or expectation, you lose your ability to be flexible and adaptable with your choices. You lose sight of what's important and true—to defend and secure what supports your current identity.

When you remove neediness in a desire and pursue it for the simple pleasure of working toward something you want, you will place yourself in a very powerful position to create your own reality. No longer will you be bound by the self-imposed rules and restrictions of your expectations; rather, you will be open to grow along with the process and to be humble enough to redirect your path when needed. You'll be more receptive to intuitive hunches and subtle shifts in perspective.

As you begin to change and become the person you need to be, your value system will also be impacted. Perhaps, the journey will change you and your desires. Perhaps you originally wanted the giant mansion in Los Angeles because it represented financial stability in your mind, but as you moved toward achieving your goal, you had an epiphany and shifted to wanting a villa in a third-world country. As you move through your journey, you might find your desires changing. That's okay. Start with what you want *now* and move forward with that. This flexibility and adaptability can only be achieved when you are no longer attached to a certain outcome—a singular ego driven version of your desire.

MISCONCEPTION: Enthusiasm is an expression of excess importance.

When analyzing most positive people, a common thread in their behavior becomes clear. They are always telling us *why* they are happy. They are continually trying to find a reason for their happiness. In turn, they begin to place their source of enthusiasm on external events and accomplishments. There is nothing inherently wrong with this. Doubling down and soaking in the energy of good confirmations is an excellent way of amplifying them. The same goes for gratitude.

However, people get attached to what causes their positive state. When external conditions become the predominant metric for an internal feeling, you become a slave to them. If something doesn't pan out, goes away, or doesn't happen in accordance with your preconceived notion of how things should be, you limit your ability to feel excited and joyful about every moment.

It is a delicate balance between emphasizing your desire and not forming an unhealthy attachment to it. Finding that balance can be difficult. Remember, when we speak of balance, we're not necessarily speaking about the emotions that are involved. Rather, it is the attributed meaning we give to the event that causes the emotion.

Say you're looking for a partner. There are two ways of approaching this. One is from a place of lack, neediness, manipulation, and importance, while the other is from a place of abundance, wholeness, honesty, and unimportance. The key is to note that both, on the surface, can look the same. Both approaches involve giving gifts, kisses, hugs, compliments, and time, but the difference is in the energy behind these actions.

It is not problematic to be joyful, grateful, giving, optimistic, or excited about where you are and where you're going. It becomes problematic only when you place excess meaning on the expectations you have. Expectations are fine, so long as you are not held prisoner by them.

Excitement is the start of momentum. There's no need to hold it in or bottle up your optimism for the journey. That goes against the flow. Joy that is fueled by optimism and not attachments is incredible. It has solid footing and an adaptable nature. It isn't stuck to one way, path, or outcome. It maintains many open avenues, and helps you grow and expand. Joy represents feelings that come from within, not as a result of external conditions.

SOLUTION: Ride the wave of good fortune.

When you experience a high, whether or not it comes as a result of external events, double down on it. Carry it throughout your day and overwhelm your environment with this good energy.

Channel this energy into something productive. It is from this space that your best work can come. It's from this space that you can positively influence people to ride the wave with you. It's infectious. When you operate from a place of abundance, it will be easier to take steps into the unknown. This high won't last forever, but as long as you aren't attached to it or the external events that led to it, you will be fine. You can even ride this high a little longer by doing something you're uncomfortable with, as it will create more confirmations or reasons to believe you're on the right path or are becoming the person you need to be. If the uncomfortable situation doesn't pan out the way you expected, you're not attached, so it's easier to assign a different meaning (one that benefits you) to it, as opposed to being dependent on it or looking at it as a downfall.

Riding the wave of good fortune has its benefits. It keeps momentum going. However, we want to be aware of the waves we're riding and if we're riding the ones we truly want to ride.

MISCONCEPTION: All desires come from you.

Most people are convinced that their thoughts are their own, but how sure are you that your thoughts are truly your own? How do you know when a thought originates from the self and doesn't come from some other place?

Every year, advertisers spend billions of dollars to influence your thoughts, emotions, and actions. They create carefully devised ads that aim to trigger certain emotional responses. They alter their images and tone their message according to age, gender, geographical location, political views, and so forth. These marketing agencies create virtual puppets that represent 'Buyer Profiles' they can use to create the conditions for their perfect buyer. Based on their perfect buyer, they create content and ads that will influence the buying choices of the highest number of people. Eventually, these thoughts bypass the external and begin to become internalized. Slogans like, "Always Coca Cola," influence the behavior of consumers to the point that roughly 10,000 units of Coca-Cola are consumed globally every second, making it the largest nonalcoholic beverage manufacturing company in the world.

Their decades of marketing efforts are why when you find yourself needing a refreshment on a hot humid day, a Coca-Cola always seems like a good option. However, this thought did not originate from within. You didn't miraculously come to the conclusion that Coca-Cola is a beverage you want to drink. It was deliberately planted in your mind by people who study your behaviors in order to appeal to your internal desires, pain points, and triggers.

It's not just corporations that implant their ideas into your head. Your government, your schools, the local church, and even your family all participate in the generation of ideas inside your head. You are born into a family where a predominant way of thinking is accepted, and, as a result, you are indoctrinated to believe the same. This includes your values, your beliefs, your ethics, and more. This energy structure is referred to as a *pendulum*.

A pendulum is an invisible, energetic structure of specific thoughts, ideas, views, and ideologies that have a set of supporters, fans, members, or followers that keep it alive through their energy. A perfect example is a football club. When a player or manager doesn't perform well, the tendency is for everyone in the fan base to go against them. When one person starts booing, the rest of the crowd follows. Even if there's no logical reasoning behind the thought, if it *feels* like they should be upset about it, they will be.

Pendulums are often destructive in nature and drain energy from their followers. The more people there are feeding a pendulum, the stronger it becomes. Its reasonings start to make logical sense, using manipulation and creating an "us versus them" narrative. The goal is to keep you hooked, so you keep feeding it. The fewer people there are who feed it, the weaker it will become.

However, pendulums aren't always bad. They can be used to bring you up, helping you achieve your goals and manifest the life you want, but there will always come a time when you need to stop feeding it, or it'll start holding you back from moving onto bigger and better things.

This is why it's so important to become aware of your own thoughts—to recognize which thoughts come from pendulums and which ones come from the soul. Ego-driven desires aim to please the masses, have more, and be more at any cost in order to accomplish a particular goal or objective. Soul-driven desires are rooted in expansion, contribution, and fulfilling work and relationships. This is where you play to your unique strengths and talents, as opposed to trying to be someone you were told you needed to be.

We've all had gut feelings before. Something inside of us telling us that we should take a chance or sit one out. When we listen to this internal voice, we typically find that it works out in our favor. However, when you go against this internal compass, you will typically find yourself on the opposite spectrum, dealing with conflict that could have easily been avoided if you simply listened to your intuition.

When most of us follow our ego desires, we are desiring unconsciously. Those who strive to achieve their goals unconsciously will always suffer their success. In other words, when the success fades or diminishes, it'll affect them internally in more ways than one. When we're able to consciously *choose* our desires, it's easier to not only put in the work to strive for them, but also to achieve and sustain them.

SOLUTION: Choose your desires consciously.

Whenever you find yourself feeling the nagging of intuition in the pit of your stomach, there are two ways you can approach it. The first is to give this nagging feeling some time to prove itself. If it shows up constantly—a day, week, month, or even a year later—this is your intuition moving you in a certain direction. If it only comes up once, it could just be a distraction. Fears of missing out or a need to please others tend to be the most common reasons it presents itself.

The second approach is to ask yourself the question, "Is this gut feeling leading me to something expansive or is it my conditioning?" Following your intuition won't always feel comfortable. In fact, most of the time, it won't. This is because when you follow your intuition, you're doing something that's helping you expand. This is how we grow. Feelings, on the other hand, are conditioned. They feel the same, like a pattern. It tends to be comfortable because it moves you away from what is uncomfortable, keeping you stuck in a loop.

When it comes to desires, there are cases when a desire will constantly come up, but you keep ignoring it to fulfill another. For example, you might have had the drive to start and grow your own business since you were young, but you ignore it to focus on the traditional path—school, internships, jobs, and climbing the corporate ladder. You may also have small desires that keep you comfortable, ones that don't force you to grow. An example of this is staying in a relationship with someone who doesn't support your big goals. If you're operating from a place of lack (ego), staying in a relationship means you're secure, while separating would lead to feeling lonely, even if this isn't true. These false truths will eventually lead you to conjure false desires. The key is to distinguish between false desires and real desires.

Whether you're operating from a false or real desire, you always need to have a desire to start off with, even if it comes from a place of ego and survival. You do not want to spiritually bypass this stage. If your initial goal for this year is to buy a new car and house, let it be that. Even if it doesn't sound like a soul desire, you have to start somewhere. As you move along your journey to manifesting this new car and house, you might notice that it isn't what you truly want. However, you'll only know that when you gain clarity from the process.

Become aware of the fact that your desires potentially come from a place of trying to please others or be seen by them. Ask yourself, "Is anyone imposing this desire on me or did I choose this of my own accord?" You can typically spot the difference in the levels of convincing you need. A fragile desire will always linger with a little bit of resistance, while a soul desire will always lead with an astounding "Yes! I want this!" If you feel a little bit of resistance, ask yourself, "Is this resistance coming from me or from the outside world?" Conviction comes from the soul. If you have conviction, but you feel like you shouldn't because of whatever reasons, then that is a limiting belief. Your soul desires are a part of you, and to ignore them because of external reasons is to ignore what you came here for—to mindfully create a life that is uniquely yours.

Mindfulness is more about learning how to listen to yourself, to discern between who you are and who you are not. It is an essential tool in the toolbox of every practitioner of the Law of Attraction. The more you can silence the voices that do not originate from your inner self and align yourself with the internal whispers of your heart, the quicker the reality that you desire will come into being without you having to force anything. Learn to listen to your internal voice, strengthen it, become familiar with it, and allow it to guide you on your path. Relinquish the need to control every outcome, and accept that if you walk in the general direction of your soul desire, you'll discover more in your favor than what you could ever imagine with the mind's limited perception of the Universe.

Some final words of encouragement...

"She remembered who she was and the game changed."
—Lalah Delia

As we reach the end of this book together, I am confident that the lessons you learned on these pages will allow you to remove the chains that keep you bound to your current reality. If you are reading these words, it's safe to presume that you understand that *you* are the missing piece. All the techniques, mantras, seminars, and books are nothing without you, the creator. Your participation and understanding of the concepts, the nature of reality, and your internal and external responses all play a role in how your life turns out.

While this may seem like a daunting thought, placing so much responsibility on your shoulders, the truth of the matter is, knowing that you have a direct influence on how your life plays out is very liberating. You are not bound to the paradigm of your environment and others' views of reality. This isn't to say that there aren't any conditioned limitations or benefits, but rather that they

do not define you or your reality. Only you have that privilege, and that is ultimately what this book was about. Together with having faith in the Universe, anything you desire is possible and already on its way. It's just a matter of doing what you need to do and allowing it to come in.

We ventured into some of the most well-known concepts of the Law of Attraction and examined them in detail, unveiling common mistakes and misinterpretations. From understanding how you must venture outside of your comfort zone to access the infinite landscape of opportunities, to accepting your current reality as it is, without judgement or resentment, we learned how making these small internal shifts can lead to amazing results. We examined how forced positivity is merely denial masquerading as positivity and that authenticity is far more powerful than trying to be someone you are not. We learned how to break out of negative thought vortexes and how to focus our actions like a laser to achieve more while doing less using your inner power. We dove deep into the mechanisms of visualization and showed you how to become one with the script of your life instead of sitting on the sidelines observing it. You also learned how placing excess importance on a particular goal leads to struggles achieving it.

As you apply these tweaks, you'll begin to notice small shifts in the way you approach these practices. The process of self-discovery will require consistent application and reflection. Even when you get results, I challenge you to keep going. There's always more to your potential. You'll notice not only how much you have shifted in your own perspective, but also how the words on these pages will take on a different meaning as you learn and

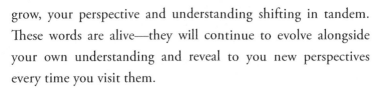

grow, your perspective and understanding shifting in tandem. These words are alive—they will continue to evolve alongside your own understanding and reveal to you new perspectives every time you visit them.

But where do you go from here? What's next?

That is entirely up to you. You now have the opportunity to either sit back and let life continue to happen to you, or you can begin asking honest questions about your life: *What is it I truly want? What can I do today to get closer to my desired reality?* Then take the simple and most obvious steps first.

Put the ego aside and focus on what the heart wants, and you will begin to shape your reality in a way that you could not have imagined. We are limited in our perception; we do not have the ability to see the infiniteness of the Universe and the fundamental elements on how it operates. The good news is that you don't have to know it all. Implement the basic principles you do know, correctly and consistently.

This book has shown you how to take your manifesting to the next level by removing the mystery behind the techniques. All you need now is to put them into practice. Happy manifesting.

A Short Message
From The Author

Hey there, did you enjoy the book? Hopefully you did! A lot of work, research, and collaborations took place to make this book what it is today. So, if you enjoyed *The Myths of Manifesting*, I'd love to hear your thoughts in the review section on Amazon.com. It helps me gain valuable feedback to produce the highest quality content for all of my beautiful readers. Even just a short 1-2 sentence review would mean the WORLD to me.

amazon.com

★ ★ ★ ★ ★

>> Scan the QR Code below to leave a short review <<

Thank you from the bottom of my heart for purchasing and reading it to end.

Sincerely,

Rynn

References

Andrews, R. (n.d.). What are your 4 pounds made of? *Precision Nutrition.* https://www.precisionnutrition.com/what-are-your-4-lbs

Market.us (n.d.). *Coca-cola company statistics and facts.* https://market.us/statistics/food-and-beverage-companies/coca-cola-company/

Pascual-Leone, A., Nguyet, D., Cohen, L. G., Brasil-Neto, J. P., Cammarota, A., & Hallett, M. (1995). Modulation of muscle responses evoked by transcranial magnetic stimulation during the acquisition of new fine motor skills. *Journal of Neurophysiology*, *74*(3), 1037-1045. https://doi.org/10.1152/jn.1995.74.3.1037

Schurmans, A. (2022) Anatomy of the Avatar. https://www.anatomyoftheavatar.com

Zeland, V. (2011). *Reality transurfing.* John Hunt Publishing.

Made in the USA
Middletown, DE
27 July 2023

35810562R00080